- CALL PRESIDENTS THAT I KNOW
  AND INTRODUCE BILL

- SEND HANDWRITTEN NOTE
  TO 3A MEETING

- CALL BROKERS ABOUT LOST
  OPPORTUNITIES.

- TESTIMONIAL TARGET MARKET.

"What a wonderful book. The only way organizations will be able to compete in the future is if their people act like owners and they create an ownership culture. A must read for the 21st century."

—Ken Blanchard, Coauthor, *The One Minute Manager*

"A terrific addition to any library. Marty O'Neill and Robert Blonchek have crafted an elegantly simple and uniquely powerful approach to enhancing the performance of any organization—large or small. I wholeheartedly recommend it."

—Douglas R. Conant, President, U.S. Foods Group, Nabisco

"The new workplace demands that businesses find effective ways to release the power of people. Blonchek and O'Neill's 'Internal Franchise' idea turns the franchise concept inside out and provides a roadmap for ownership and empowerment in any organization."

—Alan Randolph, Coauthor, *Empowerment Takes More Than a Minute*

"*Act Like an Owner* gives you a treasure map to unlocking the fortunes that lie throughout an organization."

—Bill Toler, President, Campbell Sales Company

"An insightful look at the elements of an ownership culture and how to put them to work in your company in order to attract, retain, and motivate talented people."

—J. Robert Beyster, Founder, Chairman, and CEO, SAIC

"*Act Like an Owner* gives you the tools you need to develop and empower your employees to think and act like entrepreneurs."

—Andrew C. Taylor, President and CEO, Enterprise Rent-A-Car, and 1997 Ernst & Young Entrepreneur of the Year Award Winner

"*Act Like an Owner* gets beyond the rhetoric and brings reality to the development of business leaders and creating a dynamite culture."

—Ron Charnock, Senior Vice President, International Business Group/Internetworth

"*Act Like an Owner* gives you many of the critical answers you need to embark on the long journey of developing your most critical resource and asset—your people."

—Robert S. Argabright II, President, Allpro Packaging Company

"*Act Like an Owner* is more than just a book—it's a step by step road map to the future, and a detailed blueprint for building a successful entrepreneurial culture in any company."

—Dan R. Bannister, Chairman of the Board, DynCorp

"*Act Like an Owner* should be required reading for anyone looking to take a startup company to the next level."

—Christopher M. Young, President, ProObject

*Act Like
an Owner*

Act Like an Owner

Building an
Ownership Culture

ROBERT M. BLONCHEK   MARTIN F. O'NEILL

John Wiley & Sons, Inc.
New York • Chichester • Weinheim
Brisbane • Singapore • Toronto

Published by John Wiley & Sons, Inc.
Published simultaneously in Canada.
Act Like an Owner, Ownership Culture, and Internal Franchise are registered trademarks of The Capstone Group, LLC.

This publication is designed to provide accurate and authoritative information in regard to the subject matter covered. It is sold with the understanding that the publisher is not engaged in rendering legal, accounting, or other professional services. If legal advice or other expert assistance is required, the services of a competent professional person should be sought.

Library of Congress Cataloging-in-Publication Data:
Blonchek, Robert M., 1962–
    Act like an owner : building an ownership culture / Robert M.
Blonchek, Martin F. O'Neill.
        p.   cm.
    Includes index.
    ISBN 0-471-32285-7 (cloth : alk. paper)
    1. Franchises (Retail trade) 2. Entrepreneurship. 3. Corporate culture. I. O'Neill, Martin F., 1959-   . II. Title.
HF5429.23.B55   1999
658.8'708—dc21   98-44675
                                                             CIP

10 9 8 7 6 5 4 3 2

To Lori, Stephanie, Jonathon, and Maribeth—my true higher purpose.

Robert M. Blonchek

To my life partner, Denise, and our inspiration, Jack and Liam.

Martin F. O'Neill

Contents

Preface

The business model presented in this book, which we call *act like an owner* (ALO), grew out of our experience in building information technology service businesses. When we started our first business, our goal was to create an environment that we would enjoy working in, an environment based on trust and team spirit. Having spent many years working for a large international management consulting firm, where teamwork was frowned upon and where internal competition took precedence over customer satisfaction, we were committed to a new approach.

Early on, as a company of just six people, we wrote a corporate creed that documented our principles and values—our culture. This creed simply stated that we would build a successful business by focusing on the customer, encouraging entrepreneurial spirit, empowering everyone, and sharing both success and failure. We call this culture an *ownership culture*.

We discovered that this environment was enjoyable to work in and was a powerful business strategy. We saw ordinary people, with an intrinsic desire to do their best, accomplish significant personal and business objectives. We saw the level of individual initiative and accountability skyrocket. We saw teamwork provide a competitive advantage. Our goal was to create a great working environment. We ended up with a great working environment and an organization where everyone acted like owners.

The results were tremendous. In a crowded and competitive technical services market, our company grew at a rate of almost 5,000 percent over 6 years. It was recognized as one of the fastest-growing technology companies in the country in 1996.

To this day, when we ask people associated with the company why it was successful, and why they were committed, the answer is always the same. It was *empowerment*; it was *team-spirit*; it was *vision*. It was *mutual respect* and *trust*. Most important, it was the *culture*.

This book is a distillation of our experience in creating, nurturing, and maintaining an ownership culture. Like many business owners, we studied the leading management approaches and business strategies, including reengineering, principle-centered leadership, empowerment, core competencies, and many others. The ALO model is a synthesis and practical application of these leading business concepts along with our own personal experiences. It's a model mined from research into today's leading management concepts and forged through years of personal application both in our own businesses and in consulting assignments with a number of leading companies. The ALO model is not academic theory, it's a roadmap for applying today's most important management practices to the real-world problem of building an information-era business. We discovered the power of an ownership culture in our first business, refined it in our consulting practice, and have put it to use once more at Bottom Line Staffing Solutions and CTX Corporation.

In this book, we present the internal franchise, the foundation of ALO and a framework for unlocking entrepreneurial spirit in your organization. It's a framework for managing the shifting business landscape.

An internal franchise consists of three components: an *operating model, entrepreneurial employees,* and an *ownership culture.* It's a strategy for crystallizing your way of doing business, and then turning your operating model over to your employees to run as if they own it. It's the value proposition you offer to your employees—you offer them the opportunity to become franchisees of your operating model. As such, the *internal franchise* addresses your need to focus your entire organization on execution (your operating model) while addressing the changing needs of today's workers (the desire for opportunity and growth).

The heart of the internal franchise is the ownership culture, a corporate culture built on the principles and values of the entrepreneur. An ownership culture compels everyone in your organization to think and *act like an owner* of the business.

In Part I, we vividly describe the essence of an ownership culture and its impact on an organization. Then we fully develop the internal franchise model. We illustrate how you can build equity in your ownership culture and make it part of your company's brand identity. In this way, we explore the power of a corporate culture to create an environment of shared values and goals.

In Part II, we provide a formula for creating an ownership culture and putting it to work in your organization. We address the management and leadership aspects of building an ownership culture, and we boil down the concept of an Ownership Culture to owning the word *TRUST,* which stands for:

- Teach your employees your operating model.
- Reward them based on the performance of the business and their contribution to that performance.
- Unconditionally support their actions in order to develop a truly empowering environment.
- Share information so that everyone can make effective business decisions.
- Be Trustworthy by making and keeping commitments.

In Part III, we apply an ownership culture to one of the most pressing problems facing business today: attracting and retaining skilled workers. In this way, we demonstrate that an ownership culture is powerful organizational development technology.

We conclude the book by presenting a larger historical context for the importance of an ownership culture. We illustrate the irony that throughout most of this century businesses have worked to reduce their dependence on people, only to find that as we approach the twenty-first century, people are more important to the success of a business than ever before.

Act Like an Owner will help you formalize your operating model and internally franchise it to your entrepreneurial employees. It provides the tools and techniques you need to build an ownership culture and discover its potential to positively impact your business. It is also a leadership philosophy that will help you communicate effectively with your customers and employees, develop effective teams throughout your organization, design business systems that support and enhance empowerment, create a company of leaders, and crystallize your vision for the business.

This is a book, then, about a new strategy for business success—a business strategy centered around *people*.

Our hope is that *Act Like an Owner* will be an invaluable aid for the leaders of large and small organizations alike. We believe the ALO model can be valuable to the largest corporations in America, if they understand the importance of thinking small and encouraging entrepreneurial spirit in their organizations. We also believe it is equally valuable to second-stage growth companies that are trying to become large organizations. We think the ALO model is the fuel that all businesses need as they journey into the twenty-first century. We hope you agree.

Part 1

The Internal Franchise

A franchise is a method for marketing and distributing products and services. Companies like Domino's Pizza have used franchising to grow very rapidly and secure a significant share of their markets before competitors could catch up.

In a franchise system, a franchisor licenses a business formula—a complete way of doing business—to a franchisee. The franchisee agrees to operate the business according to specific guidelines, and to pay the franchisor a percentage of sales as a royalty. The franchisor–franchisee relationship is governed by a franchise agreement—a binding, legal agreement.

The franchise model is one of the fastest-growing segments of our economy. According to the International Franchise Association, franchises employ more than 8 million people in more than half a million outlets, and a new franchise outlet opens every 8 minutes in the United States.[1] Franchising provides the opportunity to run your own business with less risk than starting from scratch on your own. One of the hardest parts about starting a business is designing the business concept. In franchising, that is already done for you. You simply have to learn to run the business. You have a serious head start on competitors who start from ground zero. Because of these reasons, many Americans are turning to franchising to pursue their entrepreneurial dreams.

In Part I, we present the *internal franchise* as a framework for putting ownership culture to work as a competitive weapon. An internal franchise is similar to a traditional franchise operation. In an internal franchise the company makes its operating model explicit and then "franchises" the operating model to its employees. The employees are then coached, mentored, and trained to operate the business at the highest level of proficiency. In an internal franchise, the franchise agreement is not a legal binding contract, it is the company's *culture*—an ownership culture.

An internal franchise addresses the fundamental challenges facing most companies today:

- A new competitive landscape where it's not what you do, it's how you do it
- A new breed of employees who want opportunity, not job security
- The inability of industrial-era techniques to address information-era challenges (processes versus people)

When you can turn to your employees, teach them your operating model, and empower them to run the business, you have established a new distribution channel. If a franchise is a method of marketing and distributing products and services, then an internal franchise is the last, untapped distribution channel for your products and services.

It offers a powerful form of leverage, not to mention a tremendous value proposition for your employees. And it's an effective framework for dealing with the challenges of running a business in today's competitive, rapidly changing environment.

Let's take a closer look at the three key components of an internal franchise: the operating model, the employee, and, most important, an ownership culture.

THE OPERATING MODEL

According to Adrian Slywotsky, author of *Value Migration*, a business design is the totality of how a company selects its customers, defines and differentiates its offerings, defines the tasks it will perform itself and those it will outsource, configures its resources, goes to market, creates utility for customers, and captures profit.[2] It is the entire system for delivering utility to customers and earning a profit from that activity. Slywotsky shows that an appropriate business design is the single biggest determining factor of business success today. This is a long way of saying that *what* you do today is less important than *how* you do it.

We agree with Slywotsky's definition of a business design, but we modify it slightly to fit the internal franchise model. Design implies making decisions. Designing a business is the process of making decisions about the key elements of your business model. For example, you decide on your target markets and customers, your product and service offerings, your method of sales, your pricing strategy, and a host of other elements. However, once you establish the design, you put it into action as an *operating model.*

An operating model is active. It is not enough to have a solid business design—you must have a workforce that executes the business design effectively. An operating model is a company's way of doing business. A business design is comprised of the fundamental and strategic assumptions that are at the foundation of how a company does things. Both are critical. Let's consider an example.

Home Depot has emerged as the leader in the do-it-yourself home remodeling and decorating business. The company has done this by developing a business design that offers a wide range of products, competitive prices, and customer service. A key element of its business design is customer service. Home Depot's success depends on providing superior service to customers.

It's not enough to make the decision to provide superior service. Everyone in the organization must understand the connection of customer service to the success of the business. They must be motivated to provide top-notch service, they must be trained to serve customers, and they must be rewarded when they do. Customer service must become part of the corporate culture.

An operating model manifests itself in the stories employees tell about what they do in their jobs. If you asked Home Depot's leadership about their business design they would mention customer service. If you asked employees about their jobs, they might say they are trained to identify customers struggling to find a product and to immediately offer help. The former is Home Depot's business design. The latter is its operating model. It is a subtle but critical difference. A business design is only as good as the number of people who can live it every day.

The first step in building an internal franchise is to explicitly identify your operating model. To do that you need to understand and challenge your fundamental assumptions about your business, your industry, and your customers. You need to make your key business decisions explicit along the customer, economic, and operational dimensions of your business. Then you can devise procedures and systems to accomplish your business objectives. You can choreograph the activities of everyone in your organization and ensure that they work together to achieve your business vision. You can devise reward systems to motivate the behaviors you need. You can teach everyone how your business works and how it makes money. You can reengineer your processes to ensure they produce the marketing result you want. You can define *how* your business works. In short, you can ensure that your business's policies, procedures, processes, and structures work together seamlessly to achieve your business objectives.

The resulting operating model is what your employees will franchise. It doesn't matter if you are the manager of a major business unit of a Fortune 500 company or the leader of an entrepreneurial startup, in today's business climate everyone in your organization must understand your operating model.

THE EMPLOYEE

When you hire new employees, are you hiring technicians or entrepreneurs? Are you hiring people with specific skills, or are you hiring entrepreneurial people with an aptitude for the job they will perform?

Our contention is that most people want the opportunity to act like an owner. But most people are never given the chance. Therefore, they are conditioned to think like technicians. Their self-concept is that of technicians. They view themselves one-dimensionally, as a salesperson, an engineer, or a manager.

It's important to begin to view your employees as entrepreneurs. And this starts with your hiring process. You can select people with entrepreneurial drive by screening for attitude and cultural fit. The entrepreneur in prospective employees awakens when you explain that they will be given the opportunity to act like owners. Then when they join your company and begin to live in an ownership culture, their entrepreneurial drive will grow, and they will begin to act like owners of your business. Your company's ownership culture becomes a *brand* that attracts entrepreneurial people to your organization and strengthens the loyalty between employees and the company.

Your job as a leader is to attract and grow entrepreneurs, or "intrapreneurs," who can franchise your operating model and execute it at a high level of proficiency. You must attract and hire people with a positive, entrepreneurial attitude and then create an environment that drives the behaviors you need. That's where an ownership culture comes in. It's your franchise agreement.

THE FRANCHISE AGREEMENT

A franchise agreement is a legal document that sets limits on the activities of the franchisee. Its purpose is to enforce the principle that what is good for the system is good for the franchisee. To the extent that the franchise agreement can align everyone's behaviors with the overall goals of the franchise system, both the system and the individual operators will benefit.

Likewise, a corporate culture enforces shared principles and values and establishes accepted behavior for all members of an organization. An ownership culture is a corporate culture that compels everyone to think and act like owners of the business. An ownership culture enforces the fundamental law of entrepreneurs: *What's good for the business is good for the entrepreneur.*

An ownership culture is a bond among the constituent members of an organization, which is cast in trust. An ownership culture implies acting and taking action with the best interest of the company in mind. An ownership culture motivates everyone in the organization to feel that they own their franchised operations, and they act accordingly. Therefore, an ownership culture is the franchise agreement in an internal franchise.

We explore the essence and application of an ownership culture, the workplace brand, the internal franchise agreement, the operating model, and the characteristics of entrepreneurial employees in detail in the following four chapters.

1

The Power of an Ownership Culture

T hink about what characterizes successful entrepreneurs. They have tremendous belief in their abilities and in their vision for the business. They have developed ways of doing things that allow them to earn a profit. They are prone to action and don't worry about making mistakes. Instead, they learn from their mistakes. They understand that when the business succeeds they'll succeed, so they focus their energy on building a successful business.

Now imagine that every person in your organization shared these same beliefs. Imagine the possibilities if everyone in your organization believed in the purpose of your business. Imagine the possibilities if everyone in your organization believed in the reward for exercising initiative in creating value for your customers and profit for your business.

When *all* employees in your organization share these beliefs, you will have created an ownership culture. They will think and act like entrepreneurs—like owners of the business. That's the power of an ownership culture.

SUDDEN IMPACT

In an ownership culture people interact in positive ways, they stay focused on winning new customers, and they collaborate. They are accountable for business results. They keep the best interest of your business in mind because it's in their own best interest.

In an ownership culture, the entire workforce understands how the company or business unit makes money and are able to identify new business opportunities. Since each employee understands the profit drivers of the business costs are better controlled. Employees have a direct line-of-sight between their daily activities and your income statement, balance sheet, or operating budget.

An ownership culture is a great way to attract and retain employees. An ownership culture provides career security for everyone in the organization by opening a range of new opportunities. Employees engage more with their jobs because they are provided with a broad view of how the business works. Their level of responsibility and authority increases and they become better skilled so that they are valuable to you and to the employment market. Even if your company goes out of business tomorrow, or your organization is restructured out of existence, your employees are secure because their skills and experience are in demand.

An ownership culture provides increased financial opportunity because employee compensation is self-funded by the success of the business. It increases when corporate profits increase.

Here are several clear examples that illustrate the power of an ownership culture.

A REAL-LIFE OWNERSHIP CULTURE

Shawn was dejected. After spending six weeks working around the clock to get the remaining bugs out of the software, the client was demanding that 200 additional changes be made to the system in less than 14 days. He didn't know what to do. How could he ask his team to spend another two weeks working around the clock? He decided he couldn't.

After gathering the team together, he thanked them for their efforts and told them he was proud of them. He told them that the client was demanding even more changes, but he didn't expect them to kill themselves in order to get it done. They had done enough. He thanked them again and headed out the door to let his boss know that they were not able to meet this final deadline. They were just too exhausted.

His team wouldn't let him do it. They believed they could pull it off. They brainstormed ideas on how to approach the problem and set into motion a plan to complete the necessary changes. Two weeks later the customer accepted the system.

Brian was intercepted by his customer on his way out the door. The customer asked if he knew a good place to buy several hundred laptop computers. Brian thought about it for a moment and told the customer he couldn't think of a source off the top of his head. However, he was sure that someone in his 250-person company would know the best place to buy them. He asked to borrow the customer's phone and left a global voice mail for everyone in the company, asking for a good source for laptop computers.

Before he could put on his coat and leave the customer's office, his beeper started to vibrate. Jokingly, he said that it was probably the answer on the laptops. He asked to borrow the phone again and quickly checked his voice mail. Sure enough, it was the answer. In less than five minutes, someone working across town had responded to the original voice mail and was able to answer the customer's question. Brian left that day knowing he had a happy customer and feeling proud to be part of the team.

Mark had just joined the company after spending several years working for a large international management consulting firm. He was hard-working and intelligent, but he had never been responsible for building a business before. However, he had a few solid ideas and sensed that the company would support him.

Over the next 2 years, Mark built a $2-million consulting business by creating an alliance with one of the largest computer manufacturers in the country. He not only found new customers, he hired almost 20 people, managed every customer engagement, and often contributed to the technical work. This alliance became a key part of the company's revenue growth over the next several years.

What's going on here? How does a young engineer have the courage to say enough is enough? Why does a team, when given the chance to slow down, agree to do even more? Why does an employee go out of his way to find an answer to someone else's question? And why is a new employee motivated to achieve tremendous personal and business objectives?

The examples described here are not the result of happenstance. They resulted from a calculated effort to nurture entrepreneurial spirit throughout an organization. They are the predictable outcome of building an ownership culture based on these five entrepreneurial beliefs:

1. Belief in the leader

2. Belief in the purpose

3. Belief in the operating model

4. Belief in empowerment

5. Belief in the reward

Let's look at these five beliefs in more detail.

Belief in the Leader

When everyone in your organization believ
leader, a high level of trust develops in you.
Kouzes and Posner studied the characteristics of admired
leaders in their book, *The Leadership Challenge*.[1] They found
that the top characteristics of admired leaders are honesty,
vision, and competence. Belief in the leader means that the
people in your organization believe that you and the other
leaders have the business acumen and talent to succeed,
and that you are trustworthy.

Competence doesn't mean brilliance. In fact, Kouzes and
Posner found that intelligence ranks low on the list of characteristics. You don't have to be the smartest person in your
organization. Competence means that you are reasonably
smart (a matter of genetics) and that you are constantly
learning and growing (a matter that is under your control).
People want to know that you try hard, make good decisions, and constantly learn. They want to know that you are
decisive.

What about trust? Humans don't instinctively trust each
other. It's not in our genetic makeup. We earn trust in each
other over time. To earn the trust of employees you must be
trustworthy. You must make and keep commitments. You
must ensure that your words and deeds are aligned with
the best interest of the business. If you make commitments
to people and keep them, they will view you as trustworthy.
It's that simple.

If people realize that the company's success takes precedence over your personal goals, they will trust the company.
They want to know that you and the company's other leaders believe that your personal goals and objectives are best
met when the business succeeds. They want to know that
they can focus on building the business instead of worrying
about hidden agendas. They want to know that they can stay
focused on the customer instead of on internal politics.

Nothing is worse than working for a manager who believes that his or her own success is a separate issue from the company's success. As an employee in this situation, where do your loyalties lie? Do you support the manager's agenda or the company's agenda? Even worse, do you now interpret your manager's actions as appropriate behavior? He or she seems to be getting ahead by acting this way. Maybe you should follow suit? The old adage that the best way to succeed is to find somebody who is already successful and copy their methods seems to apply. But does it?

If the people in your organization are spending time answering these questions for themselves, they aren't spending time serving customers. Answer the questions for them. Make sure the entire leadership team puts the company's interests ahead of their own. When they do, trust will blossom.

Belief in the Purpose

Most people want to be a part of something big. They want to share in the creation of something important. They want to believe in the purpose of their organization.

Most leading companies have a strong purpose. For example, Wal-Mart's stated purpose is to allow common people to buy the same things as rich people. Microsoft's stated purpose is to enable people to have information at their fingertips. The Body Shop promotes social responsibility. Your employees want to know your company's stated purpose. They want to know that the business is trying to achieve something that is important and meaningful. They want more than a job. They want to be part of changing the world, even if it's just their own little corner of it.

To discover your purpose, ask yourself why your organization is important. If your company went out of business tomorrow, or your organization was reorganized out of existence, why would your customers care? We often ask managers to reflect on this question. In one case, we asked a group of service managers. Initially, their answers revolved around the fact that they would lose their jobs. But after further probing, they began to open up. They talked about how they truly believed that their customers would be left in a bind. They mentioned that they often solved business problems that other companies couldn't. Without them, their customers would not be getting high-quality solutions to their problems.

Now, you can argue that their stated purpose wasn't unique, but that's not important. It was *their* purpose. That's what matters.

When all the employees in your organization share a belief in the purpose of the business, they stay focused on the big picture. Their actions align with the direction of the business. Their collective thoughts focus on better ways of achieving the purpose. They feel a personal sense of fulfillment that goes beyond just completing a job.

In order to believe in the purpose, they need to understand it. You have to constantly repeat your stated purpose as if it were a mantra. It doesn't have to be earth shattering in its creativity or uniqueness; it just has to be yours.

How many times have you heard someone in your organization say, "We need a better understanding of where we are headed."? We see too many managers thrown off balance by that question. They can't understand why people have a hard time understanding where the business is heading.

The president of a professional services firm shared his experience regarding the perceived lack of vision in his organization. He was confronted with the question, "What direction are we heading?" Out of exasperation, he rattled off a very simple, nondescript vision statement. Something along the lines of: "We are an organization that provides superior results to our customers. We are going to continue to serve our existing customers better than anyone else while we target new customers in the telecommunications industry." To his amazement, the questioner responded, "That's exactly what we need to be hearing!"

People need to know where they are going. They want to know that the things they do every day contribute to a vision. Many companies develop mission statements or vision statements. But a mission statement is only as good as the number of people who can live it every day. You need to put meaning behind the words. Identify the key words of your mission statement, and tell stories about people living those words. If your mission statement says you are customer focused, share company folklore about employees who have focused on the customer. If your mission statement says you are a team, give examples of how teamwork has helped win new customers. Bring the words of your mission statement to life through storytelling. Tell these stories to customers, partners, and your employees. Tell them to people you are trying to hire. Tell them to anyone who will listen.

Once employees understand the vision, they set off to live it. They refine it based on their own experiences. It becomes the rallying cry of your organization. Your purpose concentrates the creative energy of your people on helping your organization reach its goals.

Belief in the Operating Model

We define an operating model as the integration and interaction of your business constructs—the policies, procedures, processes, and structures of your business in dynamic interchange. It's *how* your business works.

The people in your organization constantly pass judgment on your operating model. They evaluate whether it makes sense, given their view of the world. They compare your operating model to those of other companies where they have worked, to those of your competitors down the

street, and to the models described in the business or industry literature they read.

Every day, your employees pass judgment on your
marketing strategy, accounting practices, management
approach, hiring practices, and every other aspect of your
business. Your job is to help them find reasons to believe
that your operating model makes sense.

Belief in your operating model fosters effective action
because belief is a by-product of knowledge. When everyone believes in your operating model, they understand the
rationale behind the processes, policies, and procedures
you have implemented. They are equipped to make decisions, and they frame every decision against the purpose of
the company and an understanding of business financial
principles.

Again, your job is to share the operating model with
everyone so they can inform their daily activities with
knowledge and purpose. They have to know that you take
the operating model very seriously. You have to show them
that it is designed to help the business achieve its purpose.
Talk to them about it at every opportunity. Your operating
model has to be a reflection of what you believe and what
you want for your business. It's that important.

Our mantra is: *It's not* what *you do; it's* how *you do it.* Your
operating model is really how you run your business. You
probably aren't offering a product or service that is completely unique and different. There is too much competition
for that. To be different, you have to develop an operating
model that reflects your unique vision of what your customers need. And you have to ensure that everyone
believes in its ability to succeed.

Belief in Empowerment

The real benefit of working in an ownership culture is the
ability to act on your own with the full support and backing

of the organization. In an ownership culture all employees act like owners of the business. Therefore, you authorize them to make decisions. But even more important, you train them to make the *right* decisions. Just authorizing people to make decisions is not enough—they won't act unless they feel confident that they can act appropriately.

When people believe in empowerment, they believe in the organization, and they believe in themselves. They know the organization supports their actions, and they believe they will make the right decisions. Most important, they know they are allowed to fail. Mistakes are tolerated. However, they must recognize how to learn from mistakes and avoid repeating them.

One of the authors once made the mistake of the century. He signed a $1 million fixed-price contract without checking a box to request progress payments along the way. In other words, he signed a contract that required the company to deliver $1 million worth of services without receiving any form of payment until completion of the entire job, almost nine months later. In essence, he created a massive cash-flow problem for the company.

His first response (after the tears stopped) was to control the damage. The company set out to control expenses and raise cash to solve the immediate cash-flow crisis. Then he met with the legal staff to put a process into place to ensure that the problem would never occur again. He shared the story with everyone (even though he took a lot of ribbing), so that everyone would avoid making the same mistake. In the end, the company survived and everyone learned from the experience. More important, they realized that the company could tolerate mistakes as long as everyone learned a constructive lesson and took action to avoid repeating the mistake.

People believe in empowerment when they have the authority to act, have the ability to act, and receive support when they do act. When they believe in empowerment, they feel a sense of purpose and fulfillment. Employees today want opportunities for growth, and they want to have an impact on their organization. They want to be empowered. Make sure everyone in your organization believes in empowerment.

Belief in the Reward

If you feel that salary and bonuses are the major reasons why your company can attract and retain people, you have a real problem on your hands—especially with the unemployment rate hovering below 5 percent. In this environment, when many people can go elsewhere and command a higher salary, you must give them other reasons to stay than just money. You must ensure that they *enjoy* what they do. In the current business climate, you *attract* people with competitive salaries and financial rewards, but you *retain* them by giving them opportunity and a rewarding place to work.

When employees believe in the reward, they believe that they will succeed when the business succeeds. They are willing to give their best efforts on behalf of the business, because they know that their personal success is tied to the success of the business. This is constantly on their minds. When you help your people stay focused on the big picture, they, in turn, try to improve the business so that their reward increases. They think and act like entrepreneurs, like owners of the business. They protect the bottom line as if it's their own, because it *is* their own.

THE POWER OF TRUST

The ability to trust and believe in a system is the key determinant of the system's success—even if that system is a business. If your employees don't believe in your business system, they cannot be effective. They spend too much time watching their backs instead of focusing on the customer. They spend their time trying to figure out the hidden agendas. They work *within* the system rather than working *on* the system. Politics dominates the environment. Trust becomes nonexistent. In the end, good people take their services someplace else.

Trusting the system is liberating. It frees up an enormous amount of time to focus on more important things. In this case, employees focus on the customer. When employees believe in the leaders, they adopt their beliefs and values. When they believe in the purpose of a business, they become prophets and spread it to anyone who will listen. When they believe in empowerment, they act. And because they understand the operating model, they act appropriately. When they believe that they will succeed when the business succeeds, they focus their attention on the success of the business, nothing else.

When the five entrepreneurial beliefs are inculcated in your culture, your business becomes a finely tuned system, your people a team. They believe in the game plan and focus on winning. Your business begins to operate on its own, without your constant attention. You have more time to work *on* the business instead of working *at* the business. You have more time to improve its operating model, to find new opportunities, to develop more people, and to stay focused on the changing market.

Ensure that everyone in your organization believes in the leadership of your company. Ensure that they believe in the purpose of your business. Ensure that they believe in the operating model, and that they believe in empowerment and the reward. Then let them go. Get out of their way. Discover how powerful a company of entrepreneurs can be.

2

Creating a
Workplace Brand

Corporate culture is the shared principles and values that bind together the people in an organization. A corporate culture defines how everyone in an organization acts and behaves. It sets the stage for what an organization tries to achieve. Corporate culture is born from principles but is nurtured and shaped by specific actions and reward systems. It is solidified when the organization experiences success or failure.

Mission statements and corporate creeds sometimes document and codify corporate culture. In other cases, corporate culture embodies a set of unwritten rules that propagates throughout the organization because of the words and deeds of the organization's leaders. Corporate culture lives in all businesses, regardless of whether it is explicitly acknowledged. It may not be a productive culture, and it may not be a desired culture. It may be a positive force, or it may be a destructive force. It may contribute to growth, or it may be a drag on the business. But it is a culture no less, and it is constantly at work influencing the actions of the people in the organization. The challenge is to observe it, define it, and understand its power to affect your organization's success.

The rest of this chapter describes what corporate culture is, how to identify it, why it's important, and its role in aligning people with your business goals. It also reviews research findings on the link between corporate culture and business performance and shows how an ownership culture is the corporate culture of choice. Finally, it identifies the principles and values that are at the foundation of an ownership culture's ability to act as the franchise agreement in your internal franchise, and it illustrates how an ownership culture can "brand" your workplace and help you attract, motivate, and retain the people you need.

MANIFESTING THE UNSEEN

When we think about corporate culture, we often conjure up images of IBM salespeople from the 1970s, dressed in white shirts and dark suits. We think of young, smart, aggressive engineers, dressed in shorts and sandals, working around the clock for Silicon Valley startups. Perhaps the carefree and humorous culture of Outback Steakhouse, or the formal and buttoned-down culture of an investment bank come to mind. Corporate culture is difficult to define but easy to recognize.

Often, the most visible part of corporate culture is the set of expected behaviors that the organization tends to enforce. You can see it at work when new employees join a team. Immediately, certain behaviors are encouraged or rejected. Aggressive behavior might be rejected, or consensus building might be encouraged, for example. Whatever the case, new employees adhere to the unwritten rules about expected behavior or they don't fit in.

Most of the time corporate culture just seems to evolve. In many organizations a particular style, personality, or belief

[handwritten margin notes: "Corporate culture in telecommuting" / "New ae's" / "Spend 2 to 3 days" / "center visits" / "re" / "All ee's stop" / "Teleco anytime" / "For those days." / "possibly a lunch"]

system of a key leader or leaders is the genesis of the culture. From that starting point, the culture propagates across
the organization through conversations among employees
and through actions that are consistent with the core principles and values of the culture. The culture is cemented,
either positively or negatively, when the organization experiences success or failure. Here's an example.

Not long ago, we met with the principals of a small engineering business. During our initial meeting, one of the
principals made a point of saying that their company didn't
have a culture. Everybody was just sort of doing their own
thing, without any great vision, direction, or common bond.
However, as we discussed various elements of their business, the principals told several stories that clearly illus-
trated the beliefs of their staff.

Often, the stories and folklore of an organization are the
best indicators of its culture. In this case, the principals
talked a lot about how the staff became skeptical when the
owners spent money on the infrastructure of the company.
The employees couldn't understand why the principals
would hire recruiting, facilities, and human resources staff
to create an employee handbook, establish a recruiting
process, and manage the office, for example. The employees
wanted to know what was in it for them. Weren't those
overhead people simply a drag on profits?

The owners of this organization had no shortage of stories about the interesting behaviors and expectations of
their employees. They attributed it to the lack of a corporate
culture. They were wrong. There was a strong culture at
work. It just happened to be at odds with the desires of the
leaders, even though it was a by-product of their actions.

You see, the leaders talked a lot about how they worked
independently of each other and how they valued technical
excellence. They freely admitted that management activities
were not their primary interest or strength. They also
reported paying generous salaries and bonuses, which was

a major reason why people came to work for them. Is it any wonder, then, that the employees were skeptical about expenditures that might affect their bonuses—especially expenditures on management functions that everyone from the owners down talked about as being unimportant?

The culture within this successful, growing, and talented company began the day the principals met over beer and pizza and decided to take a run at starting a company. Since the corporate culture wasn't designed explicitly, it grew out of the actions of the principals and out of the reward systems of the company. As this example shows, a company's culture is often difficult to recognize, especially from within the organization. In most cases, it remains invisible until an external event highlights the underlying principles and values, as these next two examples show.

This Integrity Stuff Is New to Us

One of our favorite examples of corporate culture is a food wholesaler in the Northeast. We'll call it Diversion Distributors to protect the innocent—or, should we say, the guilty? You see, consumer products manufacturers have a big problem called *product diversion*. This occurs when a manufacturer produces a product and ships it to a wholesaler. Then the wholesaler diverts the product into another market—it makes a profit simply by buying the product at a discount in New England, for example, and then shipping it to another part of the country where the manufacturer hasn't discounted the price. Well, Diversion Distributors made a practice of this for years and was repeatedly warned about its unethical nature by the manufacturer.

Finally, the manufacturer decided to put the squeeze on Diversion. The manufacturer threatened to stop using Diversion's distribution facilities if the practice didn't stop. It lectured Diversion on integrity, on character, and on how this practice hurt the manufacturer's business in other parts of the country. Two warnings later, Diversion still had not changed its ways, so the manufacturer finally terminated the relationship. They would no longer do business together.

Diversion was shocked. This manufacturer represented 30 percent of its business base, and it would have a difficult time surviving if it lost this piece of its business. The president of Diversion literally chased the manufacturer's executives into the parking lot, pleading for one more chance. Diversion had been conducting this unethical practice for so long, it just became part of its culture. The executives of the manufacturing firm fired back with a lecture on the importance of partnerships, building relationships, and working as a team. Finally the president of Diversion dropped his head and said, "Look, we're trying . . . give us another chance . . . this integrity stuff is new to us."

Lying, Cheating, and Stealing—No Big Deal

"Bob," a regional manager for a consulting firm in the Southeast, collaborated with Sun Microsystems on a proposal for a network engineering contract with a telecommunications firm. After Bob's team completed its initial site survey work and provided the proposal to Sun's Professional Service group, the proposal found its way into a competitor's hands.

Without Bob's consent, Sun gave his team's proposal to another of its partners and asked that company to submit a bid. Since Sun was the general contractor on the job, it was looking for the lowest cost subcontractor. Although Bob's team owned a sure-fire approach for completing the work, their bid was just too expensive in the eyes of Sun. Since the competitors had Bob's proposal, complete with costs and project specifications, they submitted a lower bid and won the job.

What we find so telling about this story is not so much that it happened. Things like this happen every day. The real story is the reaction of each organization. Sun's manager was relatively new and felt pressured to make his numbers. To him, it was no big deal to give a proprietary plan to a competing partner. On the other hand, Bob was outraged. He felt that years of partnership were wasted. His analysis of the situation centered on lying, cheating, and stealing.

This incident highlighted and reinforced both cultures. Bob and his team had long discussions about the importance of business ethics and reaffirmed the principles and values they believe in. They set off to build a more foolproof partnership model to protect themselves in the future. Sun's manager sent a strong message to his team as well. His message conveyed that numbers are most important, and it's okay to sacrifice partnerships and relationships to meet targets. One culture focused on people and relationships while the other one focused on short-term goals. Whether either of these organizations ever explicitly writes down its principles and values, their cultures were cemented that day.

WHY CULTURE IS IMPORTANT

Have you ever driven a car that badly needs a front-end alignment? Take your hands off the wheel for even a second, and the car begins to drift. On a long trip, the fight to keep the car from drifting wears you out. Over time, bad alignment causes undue wear and tear on the tires and suspension, requiring expensive repairs.

The same thing occurs in a business without a corporate culture that supports and enhances its business vision. It's out of alignment. It takes a tremendous amount of the leadership's time and energy to constantly monitor the organization's direction and bring it back into alignment when necessary. Over time, if the misalignment isn't fixed, extensive damage can occur—especially in a competitive, rapidly changing business environment. Here's one example.

Recently a mother and father took their three children to Expressly Portrait for a family picture. Expressly Portrait is a portrait studio where you can get fairly good quality pictures in an hour or two. It's an attractive alternative to both the private studios, where you often have to wait 30 days to get finished pictures, and the low-cost operations, where you get low-quality pictures.

As the couple checked out and paid for their pictures, the clerk commented on how busy it had been that day and how the entire next day was booked. She continued, saying that although the next day's schedule appeared to be completely full, there was one open slot because someone had just canceled. She had decided to leave the name in the schedule book anyway. The man joked that she was giving herself an artificial break. She agreed, but said it was the only way she could survive the day—the customers seemed to yell more when it became crowded, and she needed more breaks.

How frustrated do you think the owner of that business would be if he or she knew what was going on?

This is a classic example of misalignment in a business. The leadership of this business created an operating model that works so well it has the potential to serve as many customers as time will allow. Yet the organization is drifting away from the target. The internal resistance within the organization is costing money, *real* money. And the owner might not even know it. Just like the slow damage caused by a bad front-end alignment.

How much better off would the business be if the clerk viscerally understood the impact of a full schedule on the profitability of the company, was motivated to ensure that every available appointment slot was filled, and was trained to turn every screaming customer into a satisfied customer? And, how much better off would the employee be if she viewed her job from within this larger context?

In the current business environment, a great product or service no longer suffices—success or failure is determined by how well an organization can align, inspire, and mobilize people around its strategy. The efficient use of capital and equipment, long the hallmark of good management, must now incorporate the best use of human resources. In other words, business success today is directly proportionate to the number of people within a company that truly understand how the business works and are motivated to make the business a success. That's why your culture is so important. It keeps your entire organization aligned with your business goals.

VARIATIONS ON A THEME

In their book *Corporate Culture and Performance*, John Kotter and James Heskett explored the link between corporate culture and business performance.[1] They identified three types of cultures: a strong culture, a strategically appropriate culture, and an adaptive culture.

Strong Culture

A strong culture is easy to identify. Everyone in the organization shares a consistent set of values and methods of doing business. Accounting firms, law firms, and many federal government agencies are good examples of strong cultures. In organizations with strong cultures everyone seems alike. From the outside, the organization seems to have a style, or a way of doing things. On the inside, there is a feeling of homogeneity.

Kotter and Heskett showed that it's not enough to have a strong culture. They showed that many companies with relatively strong cultures often stumble. Companies like General Motors, Kmart, JCPenney, and Sears all have strong cultures, yet they suffered incredible setbacks during the 1980s. Kotter and Heskett determined that strong cultures keep companies from adapting. They become arrogant, inflexible, and inwardly focused. When the competitive environment changes, these companies discover that they are out of sync. They lose ground to companies that have the second type of culture: a strategically appropriate culture.

Strategically Appropriate Culture

A strategically appropriate culture is one that fits the current industry or business climate. For example, if the business climate demands quality products and customer service, those companies whose cultures encourage quality and customer service perform better.

Kotter and Heskett showed that organizations with strategically appropriate cultures outperform companies with strong cultures over the short term. But, they discovered that a strategically appropriate culture isn't enough to guarantee long-term success, either. They found that companies that perform best over a long period of time have adaptive cultures.

An Adaptive Culture

An adaptive culture is a strong culture that can rapidly change to meet new market demands. In other words, an adaptive culture allows an organization to change quickly. Microsoft's culture is a good example of an adaptive culture. When the computer industry began a major shift toward the Internet, Microsoft was not well prepared. But they were able to change direction overnight, and now are positioned for leadership in this segment of the computer industry. Their culture promotes flexibility and competitive drive.

Another favorite example is 3M, which has a reputation for innovation, creativity, and flexibility. Managers at 3M religiously try to make a certain percentage of their sales come from new products. Their culture promotes change and flexibility.

Kotter and Heskett showed that an adaptive culture is what you want. And the last two decades of downsizing and reengineering have reaffirmed their findings. Those companies that could not adapt to changing industry and customer requirements have been forced to undergo painful downsizing and reengineering. The ability to change and adapt is a critical success factor in business today. Just ask Dr. Darwin.

The Adaptive Culture of Choice

The word *change* is overused today. But change is a fact of business life. Our view is that change provides opportunity; it doesn't just create problems. It's a matter of harnessing change for business growth. Those companies charging into the twenty-first century aren't being hampered by change—they're exploiting it. They're looking for business opportunities at the intersection of changing human need and technological innovation. They're ensuring that their business design delivers value to the customer and generates a profit for the company. They're building operating models and developing cultures that breed innovation and a genuine interest in the customer. And they're doing it out of a sense of mission and purpose. That's what a corporate culture is for.

Corporate culture—an *ownership culture*—is a company's most important tool for capitalizing on the constant and accelerating pace of change. Every business owner knows the importance of flexibility—you find a way to meet the customer's request, no matter what. When everyone acts like an owner, they focus on the customer and on making the business a success. They feel empowered and in control, and the organization can thrive in an environment of rapid change.

A BINDING AGREEMENT

Your culture defines how people in your organization act. When you create an internal franchise, you want your people to act like business owners, and when you create an ownership culture based on the five entrepreneurial beliefs discussed in Chapter 1, you motivate these behaviors—you establish the values of the entrepreneur as the foundation of your culture. Let's look at these values in more detail.

ENTREPRENEURIAL VALUES

Ownership cultures value *customers*. Everyone looks for changing customer needs, and makes it a matter of routine to find new ways to serve them. IBM achieved a dramatic turnaround in 1996 by returning to a customer-centered business. Lou Gerstner, the CEO, spends 40 percent of his time with customers. If Lou Gerstner can run a $77-billion company and spend 40 percent of his time with customers, so can you.

Flexibility

The company adapts quickly to new customer priorities and market trends. It is simply unacceptable to miss an opportunity because of arduous administrative analysis or bungling, bureaucratic backbiting. Everyone in the company understands that the most potent competitor is not the behemoth—it's the aggressive startup whose teeth have been sharpened by survival techniques.

Wide Focus

Ownership cultures focus on the *big picture,* and every decision maker in the organization understands that a narrow focus can hurt the company. Here's one example.

In the mid-1990s our company had an excellent working relationship with AT&T, and we were partners in a contract to build a system for the Internal Revenue Service. AT&T had acquired NCR, so we were using NCR equipment on the project. We ourselves would not have chosen the NCR product line, but AT&T was the general contractor and the IRS could purchase the equipment at a healthy discount, so we worked with the tools we had.

As is often the case in software development, the project milestones were unrealistic. The system had to be ready for the 1995 tax season, and the time pressure was intense. During a heated project review, one of our frustrated project managers blasted the technology, declared it junk, and said the system would never work. Although this wasn't the case, the customer challenged AT&T on the choice of equipment. In turn, AT&T challenged us on our commitment to the project—and began to question our corporate relationship. At that time, AT&T's business represented 25 percent of our revenue and about 20 percent of our profits.

One parochial decision or statement made in haste to get an executive or manager off the hook can have a dramatic effect on the organization. We managed to remedy the situation, but we'll never know whether the amount of executive time required kept us from some larger opportunity while we were too busy mending fences.

Leadership

Leaders in ownership cultures develop an empowered workforce that has significant input into the direction and success of the organization. They breed and nurture a company of owners who are focused on the customer and eager to see the company succeed, and they motivate skeptical employees who don't believe in loyalty to an organization. Productive workforces don't wait for the leaders to make the rules, choose the teams, and blow the whistle. They want and deserve to join in making and breaking the rules. They establish the principles and values and reinforce the culture. Ownership culture leaders embrace this approach and capitalize on it for the benefit of the entire organization.

CULTURE AS A BRAND

A company's ability to attract, motivate, and retain highly skilled workers is critical to its continued success. Many companies replace employees at a rate that affects their growth and profitability. Worse, some companies compete for new workers solely on the basis of *price.* Higher salaries, more benefits, higher bonus payments, and other incentives all increase hiring costs. Unfortunately, someone else is always willing to pay a little more. So, prices rise even while turnover increases.

This scenario is reminiscent of the airline price wars of the late 1980s. That was the era of the supersaver fare, when the airlines competed by simply offering lower and lower prices. The airline industry almost put itself out of business.

Competition on price never works. You can't build customer loyalty on low prices alone, and you can't build employee loyalty just with higher paychecks. You have a choice. You can position your company, or you can compete. *Positioning* means value, image, and leadership. *Com-*

peting means price wars, higher costs, more turnover, and dissatisfied customers.

Position your workplace environment as a truly remarkable and unique place to work to attract, motivate, and retain the people you need. You can accomplish this by *branding* your workplace.

When we think of brands, we think of products and companies like Coca-Cola, McDonald's, Nabisco, Campbell's soup, Sony, and Mercedes-Benz. Brands are an ever-present part of our lives. Clothes, food, toys, drinks, mobile phones, cars—brands are everywhere.

Successful brands cultivate an image, persona, or personality that appeals to a specific, targeted audience. For example, Coca Cola's "It's the Real Thing" campaign was formulated to appeal to the throngs of Americans who are *original*—thus, they demand the original soft drink. Pepsi, on the other hand, appeals to a younger audience, an audience that wants to be different: They're called "the Pepsi generation."

But why are brands so powerful? First, brands nurture *increased customer loyalty.* Consumers develop a strong affiliation to particular brands. Therefore, they feel commitment, or even an obligation to purchase or use a particular brand. In the same way, a workplace brand develops a strong affiliation to your company and your culture. Your employee retention rate goes up, saving you thousands of dollars in hiring and training costs.

Second, there's *differentiation.* Brands offer a means of differentiating products and services that are, in many ways, identical. A strong workplace brand helps differentiate your company. The unemployment rate is lower than it's been in a quarter century. Competition for employees is intense. Your company must stand out as a truly remarkable place to work. Your company must become a *destination* for prospective employees.

Third, there's *pricing.* Manufacturers can often charge a premium price because of the reassurance of quality associated with a brand. Even more important for our purposes, strong brands can often undercut rivals without creating a low-quality image, simply because their name is better known or is associated with certain characteristics, like quality, style, or sex appeal. Likewise, a strong workplace brand helps you break out of the cycle of price competition. Employees are attracted to you not because of salary and perks, but because of the intangibles of working for your company—your culture.

Three important factors to consider regarding the benefits of a workplace brand follow.

Credibility

Claims about your workplace environment must be built on a solid foundation of truth. A claim without substance won't work. It's not enough to *say* that your company is a truly unique place to work; it must *be* a truly unique place to work.

Identify three to five unique truths about your workplace environment that you can easily prove to prospective employees. For example, do you empower workers? Prove it. Do you respect your workers? Share company stories that show how. Do you offer increased authority and responsibility? Let prospective employees talk to your current employees to verify your claim. Your claims must be based on truth. Everyone in the organization must believe that these claims are true and irrevocable. And this starts at the top of the organization—with you.

Customization

Your workplace brand must be customized to your target audience as well. Think about what type of employees you seek to attract. Are you filling a technical slot, or are you more interested in attracting employees who have the ability and desire to add value to the organization?

One senior executive of a consumer packaging company complained that he had difficulty attracting the very best technical talent to his organization. He had his pick of top-selling professionals because he ran a sales organization, but he never seemed to attract great technical staff for the information systems department. Talented technology employees simply did not view his company as an attractive alternative—they didn't see it as a leading-edge technology company.

If you want employees who act like owners of your business, your culture must attract them. We'll discuss entrepreneurial talent in great detail in Chapter 4, but mapping the specific attributes of your culture to the needs and expectations of your employees is the essence of building a workplace brand.

Independence

Your workplace environment must stand on its own, separate from the leaders of your organization, and separate from the specific products and services your organization provides.

Ad agencies often offer talented, creative designers the opportunity to build a world-class portfolio. This is the wrong approach. They are not building equity in the workplace environment—they are building equity in what the employee does.

As another example, a technology consulting firm attracts people because they are excited about working for one particular customer. This customer has the latest technology, which most technicians covet. However, if the firm loses that customer, where do you think those employees are going? Once again, the firm is not building equity in its workplace brand.

When your workplace brand is independent, people rate your environment or your culture as a major factor in coming to work there.

When your workplace environment is credible, customized, and independent, you have created a workplace brand.

CONCLUSION

The ownership culture is part of your organization's brand identity. It defines the value proposition you offer to employees. As such, it is a powerful way to build employee loyalty and motivation at a time when attracting, motivating, and retaining people are critical to your success.

The ownership culture is also the franchise agreement in your internal franchise. It may not be a legal document, but it's just as binding. It establishes the principles that govern everyone's activities within the organization. It provides boundaries for acceptable behavior, including exercising initiative, accepting accountability, working as a team, and staying focused on the customer. (We'll discuss these principles in detail later.) It elevates the ideal that what's good for the business is good for *everyone* in the business. It embraces the values of the entrepreneur. It is an environment that motivates everyone to think and act like owners when executing your operating model—the second component of your internal franchise and the subject of our next chapter.

3

Modeling Your Business

A model is a miniature representation of some complex system. It depicts certain selected characteristics of the system it stands for. A model is useful to the extent that it accurately portrays those characteristics that happen to be of interest at the moment.

The discipline of modeling helps you depict the important characteristics of your business accurately when you devise an operating model for your internal franchise to your employees. The purpose of specifying your operating model is to build consensus on the key elements of your business and to teach everyone in your organization about the business. Therefore, the model you build must help you achieve these objectives.

We submit that you need to build a business model that consists of these essential aspects:

- Business focus
- Economic model
- Operating parameters
- Core processes

These four areas encapsulate the critical aspects of any business. If you can accurately depict them, you can develop an effective operating model of your entire business. Then, you can ensure that everyone in your organization is working toward a common goal. Here's how:

1. Your *business focus* starts and ends with your customers. Your focus defines who your customers are and what you offer them. It defines the promise you make to customers every time they buy from you. And, you want everyone in your organization to understand that!

2. Your *economic model* determines how your business makes money. Therefore, it helps your employees make sure their actions contribute to the profitability of the business.

3. Your *operating parameters* define the operating reality of your business. They depict what your business vision really means, operationally. Therefore, your operating parameters help your employees live your vision every day, and they help you focus your investments in the business.

4. Your *core processes* are the engine of your business. They define what your business does. Everyone in your organization must understand how your business works, and they must constantly strive to improve its ability to deliver value to your customers.

Let's look at these essential aspects of your business in more detail.

BUSINESS FOCUS

When you focus you define *what* you do and *who* you do it for. It's a narrowing process. And it's one of the best ways to ensure that your entire organization is working toward a common goal. Take Starbucks as an example.

Starbucks focuses its business on giving people the chance to drink great coffee in a European-style coffee bar. They're not in the coffee business. They're in the *coffee bar* business—the business of selling a cafe atmosphere. This simple focus enables everyone at Starbucks to work together to achieve this goal.

If you are a cashier in a Starbucks coffee bar, what's your job? Making sure that people enjoy great coffee—nothing else. If you work in product development at Starbucks, what's your job? Making sure that Starbucks offers great coffee. If you work in marketing at Starbucks, what's your job? Making sure that consumers know they can drink great coffee in a European-style coffee bar at Starbucks. There's no confusion, no debate. Everyone knows the task at hand. They're working toward a common goal. The company is focused.

Focus is probably one of the most difficult concepts for many managers to accept. We often equate focus with limitations, with saying no to opportunity. Saying no to opportunity is like saying no to growth in the minds of most people. But focus does not mean giving something up. It means identifying your company's claim or promise, the benefit that you promise to deliver to your customers each time they buy from you. For example, Federal Express promises that customers' packages will be delivered overnight. Nordstrom promises that customers will receive attentive service. Southwest Airlines promises low fares.

It's impossible to be all things to all people and have a realistic, meaningful claim. You must focus. Federal Express promises overnight delivery only to customers who want to pay a premium price for overnight delivery. Nordstrom also attracts upscale customers with its customer service promise and its upscale prices. Southwest Airlines promises low fares only to customers who don't care about a full meal or assigned seating on the plane. In every case, these companies focus on a target market that values their promises.

Another way to look at your business focus is to equate it with your business purpose. Once you identify your claim or promise, it becomes the purpose of your business—the rallying cry for everyone working in the business. Simple promises like great coffee, the best customer service, and the lowest prices become the yardsticks everyone in the organization uses to measure their own contributions. If their actions further the purpose of the company, they are contributing. If not, they had better change what they are doing.

How do you identify your business focus? You start by understanding the needs of your customers.

Customer Needs

Business opportunity is found where changing customer needs and entrepreneurial perspective intersect. Changes in demographics, technology, regulations, and even geopolitics affect your customers.

As a result of change, customers become disenchanted with the status quo. They begin to consider new products and services. For example, consumers have less free time, so they look for time-saving products and services. Their budgets are tighter, so they look for value. They are more concerned about their health, so they look for health-oriented products. Corporations affected by stiff competition look for money-saving ideas. Companies affected by changing regulations look to protect their market positions or to capitalize on new opportunities.

When customers choose to buy from you, they make a *decision* to buy from you. It may not be a conscious decision, but it's a decision no less. They have gone through a process of determining which offering best meets their changing needs. This process is normally informal and often occurs at the subconscious level, but it's important that you understand it.

If you assume that your customer buys from your organization because there is a demand for what you offer, you are treading on thin ice. In the best case, you miss the opportunity to understand what customer need your offering fulfills. In the worst case, you ignore warning signs that your customers are about to shift to a competing offering that better meets their changing needs.

Have you stopped to think about what changing customer needs you address with your product or service? Do you understand why your customers buy your products or services? Are you addressing their need for lower costs, or saving them time? Are you offering new capabilities that help them maintain their market share? Are you offering an incremental improvement to a recurring operation? Spend time answering these questions. Seek the opinions of other people in your organization. Ask your customers directly. Study your competitors and ask the same question about their products and services. You must explicitly understand the changing needs of your customers. Once you do, you can devise a product focus or an operational focus that uniquely fulfills those needs. Let's look at both options.

Product Focus

Just as business opportunity is found where changing needs and entrepreneurial perspective intersect, a product focus is found where changing needs and new technology intersect. Here are a few examples.

The average family is busier than ever. More often than not, both spouses work outside the home. Yet, they still want to eat a well-balanced diet. Produce companies responded by applying new packaging technology to the garden salad. They introduced prepared salads that stay fresh for a long time. Families can enjoy a fresh, healthy garden salad without the hassle of preparation.

Companies can buy electric power from any number of suppliers because of energy industry deregulation. Innovative entrepreneurs responded by brokering electricity to individual companies over the Internet. Companies can specify their power requirements online and get the lowest possible price.

When average savers turned to the stock market as a primary savings vehicle, a huge industry sprang up to provide investment advice, financial planning services, and online investment tools to individual investors.

The question is, what is your product focus? Can you identify how your products or services uniquely meet the changing needs of your customers? Try this exercise.

Analyze your current customers. Identify the issues facing them. Engage your entire organization in answering these questions:

- What concerns do our customers have?
- What challenges are they overcoming?
- Are they trying to lower their operating expenses?
- Are they more concerned about revenue growth?
- Are they facing new competitors?
- Are changing regulations affecting their industry and their business?
- Are the consumers we sell to trying to save time?
- Are consumers looking for better quality?

See if you can categorize your current customers by the issues they face, such as new regulations or new competitors. Then, see if you can categorize your current customers based on the primary benefit they receive from your products or services, such as saving money or time. Ask yourself: What claim or promise do I make to each of my customers?

Do this analysis across all of your customers and all of the products and services you offer. Patterns should begin to emerge from the chaos. For example, you might identify a particular group of customers that uses a variety of your products and services to save money. Another group might use them to save time. These customers might come from many different industries or demographic groups, but the important thing is that they all share the same need. You want to know what needs your products fulfill, not what industries or groups you sell them to.

This analysis helps you identify the customer needs that your products fulfill. Just because you discover that your customers have a particular set of pressing needs doesn't mean that your products fulfill them. Your customers may be most concerned about costs, yet your products may promise time savings or new capabilities. They may buy your products to satisfy a secondary need instead of their biggest concern.

The last step is to identify the most lucrative areas for your attention. Once you identify your customers' primary needs and your products' primary benefits, create a simple two-dimensional spreadsheet. The rows of the spreadsheet list your current customers' key needs. The columns list the benefits that your products and services provide. Place an X at each intersection where the benefit your product provides meets the need. In other words, if your customers need lower costs and your product reduces their costs, place an X in that cell. The cells that contain Xs represent potential business focus areas.

Conduct market research on each potential focus area, and try to determine its potential size. First, identify the customers behind the need. Then identify their industries or demographic groups. See if you can spot a common thread. Are your customers in the financial services industry or the communications industry? Are they two-earner households? Learn more about your customers from a demographic perspective. If your customer is another business, how long has it been in business? How large is the business in terms of revenue, number of employees, and number of locations? How profitable is the business? Determine how many potential customers that match your demographic profile exist in the target industry or market. Identify your potential competitors as well. See if they are already meeting the need. Use this data and analysis to build consensus on your most lucrative business focus areas. Look for a focus area that has a significant number of customers who fit your profile, have a pressing need that your products fulfill, and are underserved by your competitors.

The goal of this exercise is to narrow your offerings by analyzing your current customers' needs. When you find a common set of needs that you fulfill for a variety of customers, you have an opportunity to focus. For example, suppose you discover that many of your customers worry about keeping *their* current customers. If your products and services can help them retain their customers, you have a powerful opportunity to focus your business.

When you discover a lucrative focus area, you can set off to dominate the niche. *That's* your product focus.

Operational Focus

An operational focus puts a new face on old products and services in order to provide a new class of benefits. Self-service gasoline stations are a good example.

Oil companies adopted self-service gas stations to keep their prices lower during the 1970s oil embargo. They didn't offer any new products or services—they simply changed their operations and provided a new benefit: lower costs. They did it again in the 1980s—they introduced the credit-card reader at the gasoline pump. This is another example of an operational innovation that provides a new benefit—saving time.

Let's look at how you develop an operational focus.

First, identify the fundamental operating assumptions that govern your industry. Every industry has them:

- Hub-and-spoke operations dominate the airline industry.
- Manufacturers and retailers that use promotions to increase sales dominate the consumer products industry.
- Computer companies still use a direct sales force as their main distribution channel.
- Many apparel companies still do their own manufacturing.
- Most banks still rely on bricks and mortar (the local bank branch) to expand their customer base.

When you've identified the two or three assumptions that control your industry, challenge them. It's a powerful way to focus your business.

Southwest Airlines challenged the conventional wisdom of the airlines when it adopted a point-to-point model instead of the traditional hub-and-spoke approach. Today, Southwest is one of the fastest growing airlines because its point-to-point model allows it to offer low-cost fares.

Wal-Mart challenged the assumption that you need promotions to generate sales and instead developed an every-day-low-price format. Today, Wal-Mart is the largest and most profitable retailer, because it offers consistently lower prices.

Dell Computer challenged the assumption that you sell computers through retail outlets and instead developed a mail-order concept that dominates the personal computer industry because it offers flexibility, convenience, and low prices.

Nike challenged the assumption that shoe companies make their own shoes and instead outsources its manufacturing operations and focuses on marketing. Today, Nike sells more athletic shoes than its competitors because of its marketing image.

Finally, Intuit challenged the assumption that banks must build local branch outlets. Today, banks are investing heavily in online banking.

Challenge the conventional wisdom governing your industry and your business. See if you can identify new operational approaches that let you dramatically reduce prices, like Southwest Airlines or Wal-Mart. See if you can develop new distribution channels, like Dell Computer. Analyze your operations to determine what functions can be outsourced, like Nike. See if new technology can help you turn your competitors' assets into liabilities, as Intuit is doing in banking.

Recap

Your business focus is critical to your success. Identify either a product focus or an operational focus in your business. Then ensure that your entire organization works to dominate the niche. Don't try to compete where you can't win. Don't try to grow your business by doing more things for more people. Grow your business by picking a lucrative niche, based on a product focus or an operational focus. Stake your claim to the niche and stay focused. As long as the niche is lucrative enough and your claim addresses the needs of your customers, your business will grow.

ECONOMIC MODEL

What indicators best depict the health and performance of your business? You probably already track your revenue, but what other metrics do you need to track? Here are some examples:

- Employee turnover
- Revenue per headcount
- Average sale amount
- Average number of repeat customer purchases per year
- Cost of sales
- Overhead expenses
- Inventory turns
- Sales backlog

Ask yourself: What information do I need to know in order to understand how my business is performing? What are the critical success factors for my business? These are your key management indicators (KMIs). You can find examples of KMIs by following the trade press in your industry. Also, obtain the annual reports of your publicly traded competitors. They are chock-full of KMIs.

Identify your KMIs, and you have a good understanding of the economic model of your business. You can identify the factors that control your profits, such as low operating costs, high prices, or sales volume. And you can set specific targets for the operational performance of your business, like keeping employee turnover under 15 percent, or generating $100,000 in revenue for each employee on the payroll.

Establish reasonable targets for your KMIs, based on your understanding of how your business operates. Then, determine how you stack up against your competitors. Realistically determine whether your business is able to compete economically with your competitors. If your overhead costs are 25 percent of sales and your competitors' overhead costs are 18 percent of sales, you have a problem. Develop management reports that track this information periodically. Stay on top of your KMIs.

The standard accounting ratios, such as debt to equity, return on equity, return on assets, profit margin, or the current ratio—the ratio of current assets to current liabilities—are another important aspect of your economic model.

Again, set targets based on industry norms for each of these ratios, then track your performance against the targets.

Identify the major components of your cost structure. On what do you spend your money? Is your business capital intensive? Is it people intensive? Do you have a high percentage of fixed costs, such as salary? Can you turn fixed costs into variable costs through outsourcing? Perhaps you can outsource your accounting department or your information systems department and lower your fixed costs. If you have an operating budget, review the major cost categories.

Consider the price you charge for your product or service. Answer these questions: How do customers pay for the value you create for them? Will your customers pay the price you need to charge? How do your competitors price their products? Could you price your product differently and gain a competitive advantage?

Finally, try to devise new management approaches, use new technologies, or develop new business models that allow you to outperform your competitors financially. Here's an example.

Amazon.com sells books over the Internet. This bookseller has applied new technology to an old business. As a result, its operating expenses are much lower than those of traditional booksellers that have to build and operate retail outlets. Therefore, Amazon.com can pour the savings from lower operating expenses into lower prices. And because it requires lower capital expenses, it has lower asset levels. So even if its net income is no more than a traditional bookseller's, the return on assets is much higher. The result is a higher stock price and increased shareholder wealth.

Your KMIs, your accounting ratios, your cost structure, and your pricing strategy represent the economic model of your business. If you are a unit manager or a team leader, within a large company, it is important to develop your own KMIs. Don't rely entirely on indicators your organization has developed for the business as a whole. Develop your own indicators and targets that are aligned with the corporate indicators but that apply to your corner of the world. Develop management and reporting systems to gather this information on a regular basis. Make business decisions with your economic model as your guide. And try to innovate every chance you get. The profitability of your business depends on it.

OPERATING PARAMETERS

Take a snapshot of your business right now. What does it look like, operationally? How many employees do you have? How many office locations? How many products do you offer? Who are your competitors? How do you distribute your products? Now, what will your business operation look like one, two, or three years down the road?

Your operating parameters define the operating reality of your business. They define what your vision really means, operationally. If your vision is to become a $500-million business, your operating parameters define how you intend to get there. Will you be a regional company, a national company, or an international company? What percentage of your revenue will come from existing customers? What percentage of your revenue will come from existing products and services?

It's critically important that you build a broad consensus on how your business will evolve over time. Without a consensus it is difficult to develop coherent strategies to support your goals. People will disagree on the direction of the business. Some people may believe that to get to $500 million in revenue you have to open new office locations throughout the country. Others may believe that developing new products is the key. And others may believe that you don't have to change a thing. Which path do you choose?

Here's an approach for developing a broad consensus on your operating parameters. We'll assume that you have a two-year planning horizon. So the question is, what will your business look like two years down the road?

First, identify your revenue and profit targets. Set a target for gross revenue and net income—for example, $500 million in revenue with net income of $35 million.

When you have your revenue and profit targets, specify the operating reality that will achieve those targets. First, poll a broad cross section of people in your organization. Ask them to identify the key parameters that define your operating reality today. Make sure they specify parameters along the employee, customer, and operational dimensions of your business. You want parameters like the following:

- The number and types of employees you will need, such as sales, engineering, administrative, and management employees
- The average salaries of employees by category
- The number and locations of your operating entities, such as sales, service, and manufacturing

Try to identify 15 to 20 operating parameters that define the operating reality of your business. Again, public information about your competitors can help identify these parameters.

Next, ask a broad cross section of people in your organization what they would expect each of these parameters to look like in order to achieve your revenue and profit targets. Do they expect the company to operate at 10 different locations or at 1 location? Do they expect the company to have 1,000 employees or 500 employees? Do they expect revenue to come from existing products or new products? How many products will the company offer? What markets will you serve?

When you collect everyone's input, you have the fodder for an interesting, productive, and sometimes frustrating debate about how your business should best operate and how your business should proceed in pursuit of its goals. Focus on the rationale behind each answer, rather than on the answers themselves. The thinking behind these answers holds the key to your future success. The varied perspectives and opinions of people from across your organization reveal new opportunities for your business.

Compare your operating parameters to those of your primary competitors. How closely does your view of your business and your industry match your competitor's view? Where do you depart from the prevailing wisdom in your industry? Look for ways to challenge conventional wisdom.

Consider online banking again. The institutions venturing into this new industry are simply challenging one of banking's operating parameters: the number of branch locations. They are asking themselves: What if our operating reality was based on the assumption that the number of branch locations we have is zero?

Once you have identified and challenged your operating parameters, build as much consensus as possible. Agree to disagree pending more research when you can't come to a consensus on a parameter. When you reach a quorum on the business parameters, agree that everyone will buy into that operational picture until the time comes to review and challenge the business again. Criticism of the operational picture is not allowed after you reach a consensus. Everyone must focus on bringing the picture to life. We like to think of it as democratic decision making and dictatorial implementation.

When you operationalize your business by defining its operating parameters, you define a specification for your business. The next step is to design your business processes to meet the specification.

CORE PROCESSES

Business processes enable your business to operate and achieve its goals. Design your business processes to support the operational picture defined by your operating parameters.

If your parameters specify that you will hire 1,000 people over the next 3 years, you need a very robust recruiting process. If your parameters specify that you will open retail outlets across the country, you'll need strong real estate and facility management processes. If your parameters specify that you will develop several new products, your product development processes are critical. If you expect the number of customers you serve to grow exponentially, your billing and collections processes need to support that.

The key is to identify your core processes—those processes that must work perfectly for your business to survive.

In the professional services business, for example, the core processes often include staffing, customer relationship management, and service delivery. That's because success in professional services depends on the ability to have the right people available for the right client assignment at the right time, the ability to build and maintain customer relationships over time, and the ability to routinely deliver quality services. In the professional services business, these processes must work correctly or you are out of business. They are core processes.

Systematically take your core processes apart. Break them down into key areas. Identify the critical success factors that history has shown will make or break the process. For example, we might break the staffing process into the following key areas:

- Recruiting
- Assignment
- Development
- Retention

In other words, the staffing process is really the amalgamation of recruiting the right people, assigning them to accounts that best suit their skills, helping them develop new skills as customer needs change, and retaining them on staff. In this example, history shows that if you can recruit, assign, develop, and retain people effectively, your staffing process will operate effectively. And your business will operate effectively, because staffing is a core process.

Your particular business determines the extent to which you specify your processes. Minimum specification requires that you provide flexible guidelines for each core process. In this case, your goal is to provide insight on what has worked in the past so that other people have a better chance of succeeding. At the other end of the scale, you can specify a process rigidly so that it becomes a repeatable, mechanical operation, like making french fries at McDonald's. If flexibility is not a driving concern, a more rigid specification can provide more control. In either case, you must never allow the processes to take control of the business. Review your processes constantly to ensure that they support your business—that they support your ability to create customers and operate at a profit.

We recommend the flexible guideline approach. In the current business climate, flexibility is a critical success factor. Flexibility decreases when processes are rigid and over-specified. People depend on the process to do their thinking for them. Don't fall into that trap.

When you specify your core processes, imagine that you are painting a mountain scene. You repeatedly glance up at the mountain, focus on a particular aspect of the scene, and try to recreate it on your canvas. You study the subtleties of the real scene, and incorporate them into your painting. You bounce back and forth between reality and your representation of reality. You use the real mountain scene as your guide for recreating it on canvas.

This is the effect you want from your core process specifications. You want everyone in your organization to look up, examine your process guidelines, and apply them to the business situation at hand. It is impossible to completely recreate reality on a painted canvas, but you can come very close. You can capture the essence of reality so that the painting truly inspires an image of the real thing. The same is true when you try to execute business processes consistently. You can't execute the process identically every time, but you can come very close. Your goal is to capture the essence of what works.

PUTTING IT ALL TOGETHER

When you understand your business focus, your economic model, your operating parameters, and your core process, what's next? How do you put it all together into an effective operating model? Unfortunately, there is no easy answer, because it takes leadership. We'll discuss leadership a lot more later, but for now here are the two most important things you can do to turn your business design into an effective operating model:

1. Align your business constructs with your operating model.

2. Analyze your operating model across your entire supply chain.

Let's look at a few examples.

Alignment

A mother took her son into a department store to buy him a pair of sneakers. The salesperson measured the boy's feet and discovered that the left foot was a half-size smaller than the right. Although young children very typically have different-sized feet, the salesperson's response to the situation was atypical.

Instead of selling the boy's mother a pair of shoes that fit only one foot, the salesperson went to the storeroom and brought back two pairs of sneakers. He offered to sell the woman two different-sized shoes so that they would fit the boy's feet better. *That's* customer service.

This example comes from Nordstrom, which is famous for its attentive customer service. Nordstrom's mission is to be known as the department store with the best, individualized customer service around. It's the company's business focus. Its advertising and marketing activities constantly reinforce this customer-focused image. But image and words are not enough, Nordstrom "walks" the "talk."

A company's image must be based on substance. Eventually a company's operating model must be designed and calibrated to support the marketing image that depicts the company's business focus. Otherwise, its claims seem shallow and empty. Let's go back to Nordstrom to better illustrate our point.

Think about this action of selling two different-sized shoes for a moment. The salesperson would never have done this without a well-designed and thought-out operating model. He had to be trained to be attentive to customers (even young boys with different-sized feet), he had to be empowered to make this decision on the fly, and the store's core processes had to accommodate this situation.

When that salesperson took two pairs of shoes from inventory, sold one pair, and failed to return the other pair to inventory, it set off a chain reaction of events throughout the store's business systems. The store had to send the mismatched pair of shoes back to the manufacturer and receive credit. Therefore, the store had to have a contractual arrangement with the manufacturer that allowed the return of single shoes. The inventory system had to account for the possibility of breaking two pairs of shoes to fulfill a customer order. Otherwise, inventory levels could be under-stocked even though sales levels were predicted accurately. The salesman's commission had to accurately reflect that he sold only one pair of shoes, not two. The quality control systems had to be flexible enough to recognize that the shoes weren't defective, even though they were returned to the manufacturer for credit.

The simple action of selling two different-sized shoes affected virtually every business system within the store.

It's one thing to define attentive service as your business focus; it's another thing to build an operating model that guarantees that your business provides it. Remember, to be different today you have to act differently. Your operating model determines how you act. Your operating model has to support and enhance your vision for the business; therefore, every aspect of your business operations must be choreographed to support and enhance your business model. Otherwise, your operating model works against your business vision.

Consider the home construction industry. The residential construction industry is very vibrant in the Mid-Atlantic region. You see a lot of new houses being built. Construction companies like to claim that they build custom homes. In other words, custom home building is their business focus.

They like the economic model of the custom home business because they can charge premium prices. Their operating parameters make sense as well. They don't have to build as many homes each year to maintain the income levels specified by their economic model. Therefore, their specific operating parameters—like the number of construction crews, the amount of machinery they need, and the number of subcontractors they have to work with—all make sense.

However, many builders stumble when it comes to their core processes. As a result, many builders market the benefit of building a custom home, but the customer's real experience is often much different.

Builders want you to select carpeting, tile, wall colors, lighting fixtures, plumbing fixtures, and all the other amenities up front. Then they require significant fees if you change your mind. Try to get the carpenters to build anything but a square or rectangular room, and their response can be volatile. Curved walls, windows, or walkways are the bane of the carpenter and brick mason—even when they work on custom homes. Their idea of "custom" is changing the size of a couple of closets. Obviously, the word *custom* has multiple meanings.

The problem is not that builders are dishonest, for the most part. It's that their marketing image and business focus aren't supported by an operating model. Builders know that customers want flexibility when building a dream home, so they market flexibility. Unfortunately, they haven't reconfigured their operating models to support their claims.

Builders' purchasing methods often require that they buy everything up front, with at least three months' lead time. Their scheduling practices do not allow rework should the homeowner decide to make changes after a portion of the house is actually built. Their pricing strategies don't allow for midcourse corrections. They base their arrangements with trade contractors, such as carpenters, plumbers, and electricians, on rigid specifications of activity and costs. Therefore, subcontractors have very rigid operating models. Deviations from the script result in severe cost penalties that are passed down the line to the homeowner. In short, their operating models don't support the claim of custom building services. Something has to give—usually the homeowner's temper.

Your operating model consists of the processes, procedures, and systems that span the entire supply chain of your business. It's not enough to reconfigure your operating model—in many cases, you have to reconfigure your interface with suppliers, partners, and customers as well. Sometimes suppliers are so powerful that you have to build your operating model around theirs. Microsoft's licensing agreements with personal computer manufacturers provide a good example—and explain one of the reasons for the Justice Department's interest.

Your suppliers often build their operating models around their view of your business methods, much like carpenters and bricklayers working for a builder. That's why you need a very broad perspective when you design your operating model. Otherwise, the side effects of seemingly innocuous decisions can have a profound impact on your business. The consumer products industry provides a good example.

Maintaining a Broad Perspective

The consumer products industry was caught in a price-control squeeze in the 1970s. The government had imposed price controls, but manufacturing costs continued to rise. Consumer products companies, like Procter & Gamble and Nabisco, saw their profits plummet. Manufacturers hiked their prices significantly when price controls were lifted, so they would never be caught with their prices down again. Then they implemented promotional pricing schemes and periodically dropped their prices in order to keep their average prices about the same. They would put their products "on sale" every so often to encourage wholesalers and retailers to buy them. After all, they didn't want to lose market share because their prices were too high.

In essence, the consumer products industry adopted a new economic model based on promotional pricing. But they didn't analyze the effect of this decision across the entire industry.

Over time, retailers got wise to their approach. Retailers began to anticipate promotional pricing and wait for lower prices before making purchases. They bought significant amounts of products when prices dropped and stored them to avoid making purchases when prices soared again. Retailers built their entire operating model around the manufacturers' promotional tactics. They built huge inventory systems to store products bought in bulk. They even devised schemes to buy excess goods at promotional prices and resell them in other parts of the country—a practice known in the industry as *forward-buying and diverting*.

Needless to say, this approach is very inefficient. Excess inventory is rampant in the industry. And because more people handle products as they move about in a very complex distribution system, more products get damaged and are returned for credit. Manufacturers tried to halt the practice of diverting by writing more complex contracts with retailers. The result was an epidemic of invoicing problems and disputes.

Overall, the consumer products industry loses billions because of the inefficiencies built into the operating models of companies across the supply chain. In fact, one seemingly simple change to the industry's economic model opened the door for companies like Wal-Mart to take over the industry with a more effective economic model based on everyday low prices. In the end, the consumer products manufacturers lost control of their industry. Powerful retailers like Wal-Mart, Dayton Hudson's Target division, Toys "R" Us, and several others are now in control.

Don't take your operating model decisions lightly. All the good intentions and powerful words in the world won't overcome an ineffective operating model. Your operating model determines how your business behaves, regardless of whether you like the result.

CONCLUSION

Practically speaking, you can't stop doing what you do every day and sit down to redesign your business. You have to keep feeding the troops even while you consider a new strategy. But you also need to carve out quality time to think about your business using this framework. Start by formalizing your core processes. That way you'll receive immediate tactical benefits. However, you must eventually engage your organization in an open debate about your entire operating model, starting with your business focus.

Take it slow. Identify the good ideas floating around your organization. If you decide to change directions or focus, start slowly. You need to manage your current business so that you can maximize its ability to produce a profit even while you shift your strategic focus. Profits from current operations fund your new initiatives.

Invest in your strategic direction and stay focused. Shifting directions doesn't require extensive spending; it requires intensive focus. Don't spread your resources too thin. Once you decide to change directions, put all of your eggs in one basket. Otherwise, nothing gets done. Warren Buffet, the legendary investor, believes that you should invest in only a handful of companies. According to his theory, if you truly believe that you pick the best companies to invest in, why would you put your money anyplace else? Take Buffet's advice: If you truly believe that you have identified a lucrative business opportunity, why would you invest in anything else?

As a business owner or leader, your primary job is to define, review, and challenge your operating model. But don't go at it alone. Include a broad range of people in the discussion. The people closest to the customer have great ideas. So let's get back to people—the heart of the matter and the subject of Chapter 4.

4

*Employee or
Entrepreneur*

If we asked you to list the attributes of a valued employee or trusted colleague, what would you come up with? Our bet is your list would include attributes like the following:

- Gets things done
- Shows trustworthiness
- Focuses on the customer
- Solves problems
- Exercises initiative
- Exercises decisiveness
- Displays competence
- Challenges conventional wisdom
- Understands the big picture
- Displays confidence

Our most trusted employees simply get things done. They are competent in their fields. They exercise initiative, accept responsibility for their actions, and focus on the customer. Sounds like a description of an entrepreneur to us.

Since we want entrepreneurial people working for us, where do we find them? Are we simply lucky if entrepreneurial people dominate our ranks? Or can we be proactive in attracting and hiring people full of entrepreneurial spirit? The rest of this chapter is devoted to answering these questions. We help you examine your hiring process to ensure that you select entrepreneurial people, and we point out some common hiring issues that you will encounter along the way. Finally, we address the question of what to do about employees who just don't want to be entrepreneurs.

Let's begin with the fundamental issue of attitude.

THE POWER OF ATTITUDE

Is it possible to change somebody's behavior? It is possible to *force* someone to act differently by exerting pressure and threatening punishment, but the effect is only temporary. To get someone to change from the inside out, you start with attitude. People change their behavior only when their worldview changes. The normal change process goes something like this:

1. They accept a new idea as being possible and appropriate

2. Their attitude changes

3. Their behavior changes

In other words, until people accept a new idea as being possible and appropriate, their attitude won't change. And until their attitude changes, their behavior won't change. At least, they won't change viscerally. They may fake it if that's in their best interest, but it won't be meaningful, lasting change.

Attitude is your touchstone when you hire new employees. You must attract people who have a predisposition toward acting like entrepreneurs, so you need to understand candidates' attitude. You need to understand whether they view acting like an owner as being appropriate and possible.

Can attitude impact company performance? The Gallup Organization surveyed 55,000 workers in an attempt to match employee attitudes with company performance.

Essentially, Gallup found that employees are more productive when they believe that their opinions count, when they believe that everyone cares about doing their best, when they understand the link between their work and the company's mission, and when they are allowed to do what they do best every day.

Finding people who share these attitudes isn't as hard as it might sound. In fact, getting people to accept acting like an owner is easy. Most people are eager to act like entrepreneurs. However, managers often stifle entrepreneurial spirit through restrictive policies and procedures, let alone talk to their employees about such spirit. Therefore, it may be a new concept to the people you seek to hire. But the potential is there—you just have to devote yourself to tapping it. You start with your hiring process.

AN ENTREPRENEURIAL HIRING PROCESS

Most hiring processes are biased toward identifying a skill match. Companies spend a great deal of time grilling employment candidates on specific issues such as years of experience, their credentials, and their technical ability in areas like sales, management, technology, or operations. When they find someone with a solid set of skills, they hire them. But what about attitude? What about cultural fit?

Top companies realize that cultural fit is just as important as specific technical or professional skills. They take extraordinary measures to attract and identify the rare individuals who can strengthen their teams. Extensive screening is worth the trouble, although it is time consuming.

In our first business, we hired more than 300 people in a very short period of time. As we look back at our successes and failures during that time, one point stands out. Whenever we had to terminate someone (and there were just a few occasions), it was rarely because the employee couldn't do the job. It was nearly always a cultural mismatch, an attitude problem. In hindsight, this makes perfect sense. Since we had good engineers hiring other engineers, we never had a problem identifying prospective employees with solid technical skills. Even when someone's skills weren't up to par, we could help them improve and become fully productive if they made a good cultural fit and had a good attitude. However, weak skills and cultural mismatch were always a fatal combination.

Focusing on a skill match alone is misguided. Don't look for someone who has experience managing the northeast sales territory—hire someone who has an inherent understanding of sales force management, knows how to solve customer problems, and accepts accountability for every business decision they make. Don't screen applicants for Oracle database skills—look for someone with an aptitude for database work and a desire for responsibility. Focus on finding businesspeople with specific technical skills, not just on finding the perfect skills match.

Analyze your hiring process. It should accomplish the following three things:

1. Qualify the candidate

2. Assess the candidate's cultural fit

3. Educate the candidate

Let's look at these components in more detail.

Qualify the Candidate

Most of us are familiar with this step. You invite candidates to your office and interrogate them on their skills, background, credentials, and expertise. Unfortunately, this step gets overdone. Employers spend too much time screening for specific skills, leaving little time to assess the candidates' cultural fit and educate them.

Quickly identify talented candidates who possess the skills you need and an aptitude for the job you want to fill. But focus on *aptitude*. Check the candidate's references to determine if the resume is accurate. Request transcripts and other documentation to validate credentials. This background work can be done outside the interview. Don't waste this precious one-on-one time rehashing the resume. Use your interview time to assess aptitude. Ask yourself if the candidate has an inherent understanding of the job.

Focus on behavioral questions if you screen for specific leadership or management qualities. Encourage candidates to share anecdotes of how they've solved problems in the past. Instead of asking them if they are good leaders, ask them to describe an instance when they led their staff toward a specific goal. Ask them to describe the accomplishment they are most proud of. You will learn a great deal whether they tell of an individual accomplishment, or of a team accomplishment driven by good leadership.

Use written tests to help screen for a skills match. We developed numerous tests to determine candidates' skill in technical areas such as specific programming languages, operating systems, or networking components. Although we used these tests very effectively in a technical environment, they can also be used in financial or operational areas that demand a specific competency. For example, if your organization pushes profit and loss (P&L) or economic value added (EVA) responsibility down to the division level, test candidates to determine if they understand and can identify entries on an income statement and a balance sheet, and understand how their daily activities impact those entries.

Administer these tests early in the hiring process. Explain that they will not be the major determinant in your hiring decision, but are just another factor in a series of qualifiers. This approach allows you to spend valuable time assessing aptitude and cultural fit after a quick and accurate assessment of technical competency. Southwest Airlines receives 150,000 resumes a year yet hires just 5,000 new employees. They've found a way to quickly assess competency and then focus on potential employees who fit the culture and can add value.

Assess the Candidate's Cultural Fit

When you hire a new employee, you're not only hiring someone to fill a job category, billet, or some other arcane position description, you are making a decision to bring another franchisee into your organization. You're not just hiring an employee, you're hiring a businessperson— someone who can understand the company's operating model, how the company makes money, and how the success of the company is tied to his or her personal success. You're hiring someone who can embrace your principles and values. This is your culture. The people you hire must embrace your culture.

Use the following test during the hiring process. If you can answer yes to these questions, you are thinking in terms of attracting people with the right attitude.

Does the candidate have the ability and desire to:

- Learn your operating model?
- Execute your operating model?
- Teach your operating model?

A candidate's willingness to spend the time and effort to learn your operating model sets the stage for his or her ability to make sound business decisions once hired. If each employee understands what the company does and how the company does it, everyday actions are translated directly into top-line revenue gains or bottom-line profits. Finally, when an employee develops the ability to teach the operating model to new employees, your way of doing business is reinforced. One generation of employees sees to it that the next one understands the operating model and thus perpetuates your way of doing things.

Ask yourself two more questions. Does the candidate have the ability and desire to:

- Challenge your operating model?
- Improve your operating model?

Your competitive position is destined to change. There is certainly no sign that competition is lessening, or that your products and services will succeed without changing. Customers continue to ask what you have done for them lately.

Spend most of the interview asking candidates probing, leading questions that help you assess their ability to fit into an ownership culture. Consider using small teams when interviewing candidates. People relate differently in group sessions than they do one-on-one. Ask them questions about their experiences working closely with customers. Determine if they are motivated by helping customers. Ask them to tell you stories about their experiences working in teams. Ask them about innovative ways they have improved their current company's ability to perform. Focus on their goals and aspirations. Are they interested in learning how your business runs? Do they take accountability for their actions? Their answers indicate how well they will fit in.

Educate the Candidate

This step occurs in every interview, even if you decide that the candidate is not a match. Every candidate must leave your organization wanting to work for your company. Most candidates want to work for an innovative, market-leading company—make your company a *destination* for prospective employees.

A friend and colleague of ours, Carter Glass, said it best. In the current job market, which is a seller's market, the smart companies don't interview anymore—they sell. He's right. Look at the interviewing process as an opportunity to sell your value proposition to prospective employees.

Deliver a stump speech to every prospective employee. Remember, attitudes change when people accept something new as being possible and appropriate. Your first interview with a prospective employee is the best time to start explaining what is appropriate and possible in your organization, to start affecting their attitude. Spend some time explaining the specific job or role you seek to fill. Most people want to know about that. Describe the basics like benefits, vacation time, and so forth. But spend most of your time talking about your culture. Sell your culture by being able to truthfully say that everyone in your organization:

1. Is given the opportunity to do what they do best every day

2. Believes their opinions count

3. Is committed to doing their best

4. Understands the link between their work and the company's mission

When these attitudes are real in the minds and hearts of your employees and prospects, every prospective employee will go back to friends and colleagues saying, "You won't believe the company I interviewed with today."

We repeat: Most people want to work in this kind of environment. Talk to prospects about your innovative programs to develop leaders at every level in the company. Tell them about the intangible elements of the work environment. Explain the higher purpose everyone shares as employees of the company. The entrepreneur in them will awaken— their eyes will light up, and their attitudes will begin to change. When they join your company they will be ready to act like owners.

INTERMEZZO—THE PAYOFF

We once invited Peter Schutz, the former CEO of Porsche, to a leadership retreat. Peter shared a number of his management and leadership philosophies, but one hit home. Peter had joined Porsche during a time of low profitability and even lower morale. In his first few weeks with the company, Peter met with the team responsible for Porsche's entry in the Sebring auto races. Peter asked what the team's chances were for winning an upcoming race. To his surprise, the team pronounced that they had no chance. They had entered the race only for promotional purposes and to test some new technology. In a somewhat knee-jerk yet brilliant reaction, Peter proclaimed that Porsche would never again enter a race but for the sole purpose of winning. He demanded that they go off and determine how they were going to go about winning the race. They were to come back at 10 A.M. the next day with a plan.

The results were dramatic. Soon after word leaked out, Peter began receiving calls from world-class drivers who wanted to join the team now that Porsche was committed to winning. The engineering team came up with creative ways to piece parts of various Porsche models together in order to make a real splash in the race. High-initiative, team-oriented, and goal-driven people were attracted to the Porsche team because they sensed a change and they wanted to be part of it.

As you change your hiring process to screen for entrepreneurial spirit, the word will begin circulating in your industry. People who are biased toward action and genuinely excited about the opportunity to work for a company that values entrepreneurial spirit will seek you out. Highly competent people who have become frustrated with their current employment situation will target you as an employer of choice.

HIRING ISSUES

Obviously, not everyone thinks this entrepreneurial stuff is a great idea. Some people just don't fit into this system. We found that senior-level people, those who were ready for that promotion to vice president and who were looking to join our company to nab that title, didn't buy our "radical" approach. We even heard comments like, "Socialism was proven not to work." On the other hand, people looking for opportunity came knocking on our door. People looking for a highfalutin position were turned off. But that's okay. We wanted that.

The "corporate ladder" loses its significance in an ownership culture. As Jack Welch says, "If you spend any of your time with your face toward the company . . . your rear-end is turned toward your customer." That's not a pretty sight! Entrepreneurs are driven by action. They're not concerned with corporate politics. They care about what they offer to their customers. They're focused on keeping their customers satisfied and on earning a profit.

Titles become less significant when less emphasis is placed on the organizational structure and less energy is spent climbing the corporate ladder. Entrepreneurial employees begin to realize that their self-worth is not wrapped up in their job title.

Corporate life changes in an ownership culture. Prospective employees who have spent time in organizations that embrace a more traditional, hierarchical career ladder are often uncomfortable in the beginning. But stick to your principles. You want people to join your company for one reason: They want to succeed by acting like owners and contributing to the growth of your business.

FALLOUT

What about people who just don't want to be entrepreneurs? Some people in your organization were very comfortable with the way things were. Some employees start out resistant to change, but adapt and grow when they see additional opportunities. Others are more than happy keeping their heads down and never worrying about what the customer thinks. They can't imagine tying their compensation to their performance—or, worse yet, to the company's performance. Fortunately, most people respond very positively when leaders decide to increase initiative, accountability, and customer focus.

The requirement that all parts of the team pull their weight and contribute to the overall success of the organization puts subtle yet constant pressure on everyone. Those who are excited about embracing the entrepreneurial spirit succeed. Those who constantly fight the changes are ultimately rejected by the culture.

We had a very early lesson as business leaders when we had the unpleasant task of firing one of our first team members. He had initially been a productive member of our small team but as we began to grow in size and mature in our abilities, his desire to adapt seemed to stop. He focused on his own objective instead of the customer's requirements. He willfully developed his own standards, rather than sticking to the protocol the team had agreed upon. He began to hide valuable information in an environment where everyone embraced sharing information for the good of the team.

After a number of counseling sessions, we let him go. To our relief and surprise, a number of other team members told us they had been wondering when we would get around to terminating him. The team had already "fired" him and built walls around him to ensure that his counter-entrepreneurial ways would not endanger the success of the project. Our strong ownership culture had already rejected him before we officially fired him.

Expect some fallout when you create an ownership culture and a workforce of entrepreneurs. Your strong culture will help filter out the few malcontents, and it will also help change a few of them. Peer pressure is a powerful motivator. When employees teeter on the cusp of acceptance and see everyone else acting like owners, the urge to give it a try can be overwhelming.

Occasionally, you'll see employees who are compliant with the culture but not committed to it. They don't openly fight it, but they don't completely buy into it, either. That's okay. Simply explain that they are required to understand how the business works and how their actions contribute to the business as a standard part of the job. That's the minimum you expect—everyone working toward the same goal.

CONCLUSION

Hiring and firing people until you find the rare superstar won't work. Create hiring processes that target entrepreneurial people. Create an environment that encourages entrepreneurial employees to look for opportunities. Attracting entrepreneurial employees gives you a significant competitive advantage. An entrepreneurial workforce executes your operating model and makes the internal franchise a success.

Devise a hiring process that tests for cultural fit. Teach prospective employees about your culture as early as their first interview and be prepared that some people just won't buy it. Early identification of the right aptitude and attitude is critical. Some people will revolt. Don't be naïve; expect some fallout. Also expect to spend significant time convincing people that it is possible and appropriate to act like an owner. Be persistent. It will pay off in spades.

Part 2

The Law of the Harvest

The farmer is solely accountable for the harvest. There's nobody else to blame. If the harvest is unproductive, the farmer can't blame the seed. If the climate and environment turn harsh, the farmer has to react as best he or she can, relying on experience and intuition. And more important, the farmer has to prepare for bad times. Sooner or later a drought will hit. The farmer had better be prepared. That's the *law of the harvest*.

The law of the harvest is a perfect metaphor for the process of building an ownership culture. As we discussed in Part I, an ownership culture is the central component of the internal franchise. It is the franchise agreement. Your ownership culture compels everyone to think and act like an owner of your business. Part II presents a formula for creating an ownership culture. We help you do the right things so that an ownership culture takes root in your organization.

Chapter 5 addresses the notion of cultivating the corporate soil. The corporate soil is your corporate culture, and your specific words and deeds determine if you have an ownership culture. It starts at the top of the organization. We identify the key management actions that cultivate an ownership culture.

Chapter 6 addresses the importance of compensation in motivating behavior that is consistent with an ownership culture. We help you develop compensation programs that reward employees based on the performance of the organization and the individual contribution of each employee.

Chapter 7 identifies the four key behaviors that are the first signs that an ownership culture is taking root.

Chapter 8 addresses the importance of leadership in an ownership culture, and we present an effective leadership model that will help you nurture your ownership culture once it begins to take hold. An ownership culture is all about leadership.

Chapter 9 focuses on the harvest. We show you how an ownership culture can positively affect company performance, and how to measure its impact on your own business. We also illustrate how you can get everyone in your organization to create a line of sight between their everyday activities and your income statement and balance sheet.

Obeying the law of the harvest in business means cultivating the corporate soil (creating an ownership culture), planting the seeds (empowering your employees), watching for the first signs of growth (the key behaviors), and nurturing the crop (leadership). When you follow these steps, you reap an abundant harvest.

5

The Seeds or
the Soil?

The number of people who have been laid off, know someone who has been laid off, or at least have read and heard reports about layoffs is staggering. You would have to have been living in a monastery in Tibet for the last 15 years to avoid being influenced by the changing employment situation in the United States. Even with unemployment at record lows, we all know that job security is a rare commodity today.

Not long ago, workers expected lifetime employment from their employers. Corporate policies and union contracts often prescribed lifetime employment for those people who made it to work every day on time, did the right things, and generally kept their noses clean. But this implicit employment contract has been nullified after more than two decades of layoffs, downsizing, and reengineering.

We see the perceived lack of employee loyalty and commitment as a side effect of the fact that companies try to enforce the old employment contract when it is obvious that it is no longer valid. When a company says, "Just do your job and we will take care of you," the employees say, "Prove it." This isn't a sign of a lack of commitment or loyalty, it's a sign of common sense. Workers aren't going to fall for that one again.

Employees now know that companies can't and won't provide job security, and they know that their career security starts and ends with themselves. They are willing to take more responsibility for their careers, but in return they want more control over their own destinies—they want more opportunity. In fact, any company that offers job security is viewed with skepticism. Employees know better. They understand that the opportunity to grow personally and professionally is the cornerstone of long-term career security.

A New Contract

A new implicit employment contract is emerging. It specifies opportunity in exchange for initiative. The employee gets the opportunity to grow professionally and personally in exchange for exercising initiative in creating value for the customer and profit for the company. Employees' jobs become more fulfilling, more rewarding, and more difficult. They learn more about how the business runs and how decisions impact the company's performance. They have a more direct impact on the performance of the business, and they have more responsibility and accountability for the company's performance. In return, the business seeks higher levels of initiative, accountability, and customer focus from its workers.

It's the perfect quid pro quo. The business succeeds because the customer is satisfied. The employees succeed because a successful, growing organization creates opportunity, and helps them develop valuable business skills that keep them competitive in the job market. It is a positive, reinforcing, and symbiotic relationship, and it is a noticeable departure from the traditional employee–employer relationship that has been characterized by internal competition, mistrust, and malaise.

When you stop to think about it, it's amazing that the old model worked for as long as it did. For most of this century, senior management hired scores of middle managers and supervisors to watch the employees and ensure that they fulfilled their end of the bargain—that they did what they were told. Workers, on the other hand, unionized so that they could keep management honest. Their union contracts ensured job security and a growing standard of living, regardless of whether the business climate or the company's performance allowed it.

A changing business environment has exposed the weaknesses of this approach, but in hindsight, how could American businesses have viewed this environment of mutual mistrust as an effective way to operate in the first place? It's not natural.

The old contract worked in an era of high demand, limited competition, and expensive technology because the company was in control. The consumer had few choices. In an era of global competition, cheap and accessible technology, and tight labor markets, using the old model is the death knell of business failure.

Today, the customer is in control. Successful companies need to be fast, focused, flexible, and friendly. The current business climate demands a complete focus on the customer and an ability to change direction overnight. The entire organization must work together to create customer value to compete in this environment. The old model of mistrust and internal competition no longer works—it diverts critical energy and attention away from the customer.

A NEW WORKPLACE ENVIRONMENT

An ownership culture can be infused into any business. It doesn't require new employees; it requires a change in the workplace environment—a new culture. The new culture

must meet the needs of the new implicit employment contract.

   Building an ownership culture is a matter of establishing
a set of principles and values that encourage an ownership
mentality, constantly communicating them, and ensuring
that reward and incentive programs reinforce them. When
you combine an ownership culture with an effective operating model and your entrepreneurial employees, business
success isn't far behind. Let's look at how you can create an
ownership culture in your organization.

BUILDING AN OWNERSHIP CULTURE

We offer a simple mnemonic to help you remember the
actions and activities that enable you to create an ownership
culture in your company. The mnemonic is TRUST:

Teach

Reward

Unconditional support

Sharing information

Trustworthy

Let's look at each of these components in detail.

Teach

We have worked closely with a variety of companies in all
phases of corporate development while writing this book.
Some are medium-sized growth companies that have successfully made it through the startup phase. Others are
more established businesses that are looking for ways to

encourage growth. Still others are large organizations that have become slow-moving behemoths and are searching for ways to reignite the entrepreneurial spirit.

Almost without exception, the successful organizations we work with, large or small, share two common characteristics. First, they have developed a unique way of attracting customers. Second, they ensure that everyone in their entire organization knows exactly how the company operates. Let's explore why both components are critical.

Not long ago we met with a gentleman who joined a rapidly growing technical services organization after being laid off from a large computer equipment manufacturer. He set out to document his way of doing business when he was laid off, instead of worrying about what he would do next. He developed a nice presentation that described how he had successfully generated business in the technical services market, and he went out and sold it to several companies. It was his personal operating model, and it was terrific. In no time, he had several job offers, and he picked a company that he wanted to work for. But he stopped there.

When we spoke with him, he was struggling with the rapid growth that his operating model had created. He was feeling overwhelmed and concerned about the future, even though he knew that the opportunity was tremendous. He wasn't confident that the people reporting to him were capable of executing his operating model. We asked him one simple question: How many of your team members understand your personal operating model as well as you do? The silence was deafening. He hadn't thought about teaching the formula to anyone else. Is there any wonder why the people on his team were less effective than he was?

Developing an effective operating model is only half the battle. That's why successful companies also ensure that everyone in the organization, starting with the leadership team, understands how the business works. For example, Bill Toler, president of Campbell Sales Company, describes his job as having two major components: Spending time in the marketplace, and teaching the next generation of leaders how Campbell works. Jack Welch spends 30 percent of his time developing leaders at General Electric, according to Noel Tichy in his book *The Leadership Engine*.[1] There is no better use of your time as a leader than teaching the next generation of leaders how your company works.

Many companies never realize their full potential because the transfer of knowledge runs smack-dab into a limited span of control. Fortune 500 companies flounder because even the most innovative strategies die when second-, third-, and fourth-generation leaders struggle with what it means to implement these ideas.

Since 1996, almost every consumer products company in the country has adopted some form of "return" concept. Whether it is called economic value added (EVA), return on investment (ROI) or return on invested capital (ROIC), the idea is to engage everyone in activities that have a positive impact on the company's value.

All this sounds great. No one is a bigger proponent of aligning business activity with value-added results than we are. We couldn't be happier that large companies are beginning to push these concepts deep into their organizations. The problem that has popped up, however, is that concepts like EVA, ROI, ROIC, and P&L don't always translate well into employee actions that make a difference.

The companies that successfully implement these strategies are the ones that can draw a line of sight between the daily activities of all employees and the indicator they are tracking, like EVA. Those that don't are relegated to the management-theory-of-the-month club, where employees sit back and say, "If I just keep my head down for the next two months, this, too, will pass." The missing link between management theories and successful implementation is education grounded in a solid understanding of business financials, as the next example shows.

Bob Augerbright was one of the leaders of the open-book management movement and is president of AllPro Packaging. Bob ran the Chesapeake Packaging facility in Baltimore in the early 1990s. He loves to tell the story of winning a corrugated box contract with the McCormick spice company not because of great selling techniques, but because he created a well-trained workforce that understood exactly how Chesapeake Packaging operated.

After Bob took over Chesapeake's Baltimore facility, word began seeping into the business community that he was teaching all of his employees how Chesapeake Packaging made its profits. All employees understood how their jobs and daily activities affected the income statement and balance sheet of the company. Employees knew how they fit into the overall operations of the organization, and they could tell you what impact they had on the company's bottom line.

Chesapeake Packaging was also developing a very good reputation for customer service. The entire workforce understood that since there isn't much to differentiate you when you make boxes for a living, how you do your job takes on even more importance. For example, employees in the plant understood the importance of quality, just as those in distribution understood the need for on-time deliveries.

McCormick heard about Bob's management of the facility, so some executives scheduled a plant tour to have a look for themselves. Much to their surprise, Bob didn't give them the tour. One of the operators from the shop floor took the McCormick executives for a 90-minute tour of the facility and explained the company's operations in detail.

The McCormick executives were convinced. There were no sales presentations, no discussion of terms and agreements, and no haggling over discounts and delivery schedules—just the opportunity to do business with a box supplier whose entire workforce understood that a company succeeds when the customer is happy, and understood exactly how to contribute to customer satisfaction.

Ignorance, Not Negligence

A wise (but confusing) old man once said, "What you know won't hurt you, and what you know you don't know won't hurt you, but what you don't know that you don't know will kill you." This sums up the decision-making ability of well-intentioned and underinformed employees. They do the best possible job that they know how to do. And chances are they make good decisions if they have all of the necessary information. So it's up to you, as a business leader, to ensure that your employees have the necessary information and insight into your operating model.

Imagine that an employee is negotiating on his or her own for the first time. Through word of mouth, informal hallway discussions, and other indirect ways, the employee discovers that the company always makes money when the spread between the bid price and the estimated cost of a product or service offering is at least 20 percent. In other words, the company's overhead and administrative costs are less than 20 percent, so the company makes a profit at a price point that provides a 20 percent gross margin on each sale.

Armed with this information and eager to get the business, the employee works hard to negotiate that 20 percent margin. Unfortunately, information the employee does not have shows that he or she could easily have asked for a gross margin of 30 percent. The market would easily have supported the higher price. In this situation, the employee missed the opportunity for an additional 10 percent profit. Did the employee do the right thing? Of course. Did it hurt the company? Of course. These well-intentioned mistakes can slowly kill an organization, and they occur all the time.

Education

The only answer to this problem is education. All employees who have the authority to make business decisions must completely understand the company's operating model. They must understand the fundamental and strategic assumptions underlying the operating model as well as—or better than—the business owner does. They must understand how the company makes a profit and the major cost drivers of the operating model. It is the responsibility of the company's leadership to provide this education.

Whenever costs seem to be getting out of control, or productivity seems to be falling, look first at how well the decision makers in the organization understand the operating model. Most of the time, underperformance is the result of ignorance, not negligence.

Many managers, when faced with declining performance, make the mistake of relying on processes and procedures to fix things. Conventional wisdom says that businesses should develop new policies, procedures, and processes to control growth and manage profitability. But conventional wisdom is dead. A command-and-control mentality is a product of the industrial era and no longer works in the information era. Indeed, growth and profitability have never come from new policies, procedures, and processes alone. So why do so many managers fall back on such traditional constructs when faced with performance problems? Why do so many Fortune 500 executives rely solely on their monthly and quarterly management tools rather than proactively coaching and mentoring their next generation of leaders? Let's explore a couple of reasons.

Many entrepreneurs in startup organizations mistakenly believe that the business acumen and talent of the original founders and leaders of the organization can be captured in policies, procedures, and processes. But even if it were possible to pull the business model out of the heads of the founders and design ways to implement it, a process or procedure isn't flexible enough to handle the rapid pace of change in the current business climate.

Employees in large companies also must understand their ability to impact the organization's bottom line. For example, McCormick uses a significant amount of pepper in manufacturing their seasoning. The pepper comes in big 50-pound bags, and warehouse workers move them around on pallets with forklifts. The profit from the sale of several thousand cans of seasoning is lost if one of those bags is destroyed in handling. It's that dramatic.

You must teach your people about the performance factors that affect your profitability. Most companies are lucky if they earn 5 to 10 cents in profit on every dollar of sales. Your margin of error is therefore very small. People must perform at peak levels in order for you to earn a profit. It's that important.

Herd mentality is another reason why many managers rely on processes instead of on teaching. When the leaders of an organization begin to feel the negative effects of change, they instinctively look at other organizations that have experienced rapid change and try to copy their methods of dealing with it. But the available models are tired, industrial-era approaches that focus on implementing new processes and procedures. As a result, the entire enterprise turns inward. The organization begins to create processes, policies, and procedures faster than it creates customers. And that is the death knell of entrepreneurial spirit within any organization, large or small.

Companies need a new model for dealing with growth in the information age. We propose the internal franchise model. The internal franchise model balances processes and people. Processes are not an end in themselves; they become tools that empowered business owners use to provide value to customers. The important thing is to *teach* people how the business works and how to leverage processes and procedures to do things better, faster, and easier.

We provided a framework for exploring the fundamental and strategic assumptions of your business in Chapter 3. Use this framework to teach your employees. Engage them in broad discussions about your business and how it works. Seek their opinions on how to make the business work better. Make sure they understand the key operating specifics of your business, and then turn them loose. Your ability to improve your performance depends on it.

Reward

As we mentioned before, all successful entrepreneurs understand the inextricable tie between business performance and personal success. When the business succeeds, the entrepreneur succeeds. If the business fails, the entrepreneur fails. Smart entrepreneurs stay focused on making the business successful. Their personal success depends on it.

The law of the entrepreneur should govern the design and implementation of your reward system. Your reward system must motivate everyone to stay focused on making the business successful. In an ownership culture, everyone must understand the link between business success and personal success, even though everyone defines success differently.

Some people view success as making a lot of money. Others view success as working with people they enjoy. Some people view success as a challenging assignment, or the opportunity to grow professionally and personally. Still others view success as maintaining balance in their lives— being able to go home and spend time on a hobby or with their family. No matter how people define success, they must see the connection between the success of the business and their ability to achieve personal goals. We devote all of Chapter 6 to the subject of devising an effective reward system.

Unconditional Support

Empowerment is a trendy concept today. When people are empowered, they are granted authority. This doesn't mean that they will *act* on that authority.

The preconditions of empowerment include the authority to act, the ability to act appropriately, and the freedom to make mistakes. Employees must believe that they have the authority to act, that they have enough information and knowledge to act appropriately, and that the organization supports them when they do act. Without the presence of all three preconditions, empowerment remains an empty promise.

If you grant authority and educate your staff, the freedom to make mistakes is the catalyst for true empowerment—empowerment with a purpose. Your employees are empowered to execute your operating model. They are franchisees of the business.

We all make mistakes. It's one of the best ways to learn. In the book *Empowerment Takes More Than a Minute*, Blanchard, Carlos, and Randolph say: "Every *misteak* is an opportunity to increase competence."[2] As business owners and leaders, we take this for granted. We need to extend this privilege to our empowered employees.

Treat mistakes as tuition payments, as the cost of higher education. There is a real price for education, and it is expensive.

It's no different in the business world. Learning is valuable, but it has a cost. When someone makes a mistake, money may be lost or a relationship with a customer may be damaged. The key is to learn from mistakes. Then you and your employees can view mistakes as an investment, as tuition payments.

Analyze your company's mistakes as enthusiastically as you celebrate your successes. Make it a rule to publicly analyze and discuss all major mistakes, so that everyone can learn from them. Reward employees who exercise initiative, even if their actions result in a mistake. Publicly praise those employees who make a mistake and take it upon themselves to teach others how to avoid it in the future.

Set the example yourself if you hold any kind of traditional leadership role in the company. The next time you blow it, let the company know about it. Publicly explain what your mistake was, why you made it, and how you will ensure that you won't make it again. Show everyone that you take mistakes seriously, that you take responsibility for the error, but that life goes on. Most mistakes aren't fatal by themselves; it's the repeated occurrence of the same mistake that hurts. That's where you draw the line.

Tolerate mistakes only if they are made with good intentions and if everyone learns from them. Good intentions alone aren't enough—you still need results. Learning occurs only when everyone shares mistakes, and mistakes are shared only when the organization supports initiative gone amok.

Avoid mistakes whenever possible, tolerate them when they are made, and ensure that they are not repeated. This is the key to creating an empowered workforce.

Sharing Information

Vince Lombardi, the legendary coach of the Green Bay Packers, reportedly offered his playbook to any opposing coach who wanted it. His philosophy was that execution would determine his team's success even if the opposing team knew all his plays. Lombardi realized that hiding information doesn't make it valuable—using it appropriately makes it valuable.

The same is true of most corporate information. Little of the information that management keeps so close to its vest is dangerous in the hands of employees. In fact, it's dangerous only when it's *not* in their hands. Teach your employees to handle proprietary information, except for bona fide trade secrets on a par with the recipe for Coca-Cola. Use the rule of thumb that employees should see all information that they are mature enough to handle appropriately. In other words, if employees can objectively use information to make better business decisions, give it to them.

Open communication means *open*—everything, the complete picture, all the time. The only rule should be, *protect the privacy of the individual.* Don't share personal financial information unless it is absolutely critical to do so. Control who has access to that type of information. Share everything else.

Managers often rely on several myths to rationalize the need to hide information when in reality they are just trying to stay in control through selective information sharing. Some typical myths follow:

- *Competition.* If I give them that information, it will wind up in the hands of our competitors.
- *Prices.* If I tell them what we charge our customers for our products or services, they will demand a pay increase.
- *Bad news.* If I tell them our market share is decreasing, it will negatively affect morale.
- *Financial information.* If I show them the income statement and balance sheet, they'll ask tough questions.
- *Employee feedback.* Once-a-year performance reviews are sufficient.

Let's look at these five myths a little more closely.

Competition

Your competitors already have all the information they need about you. They can get a tremendous amount of information about you from perfectly legal sources. Former employees, former partners, suppliers, and customers all remain more than willing to talk about you. And because of the impact of information technology, the flow of business information is almost unrestricted. The stock market is a great example.

Companies traditionally release press statements about earnings, business strategies, and other corporate news after the markets have closed, especially if they have bad news to report. The hope is that news spreads more slowly if it is released after most investors have gone home and are focused on more important things than the stock market. But this approach rarely works today.

Because of the newswire services, the Internet, and other sources of financial information, all news spreads instantaneously. Companies that try to slip bad news out in the middle of the night are often shocked when their stock's opening price already reflects the bad news the next day.

Adopt Vince Lombardi's attitude: It's not what you know, it's what you do with it. Don't worry about information getting into your competitors' hands—worry about information not getting into your employees hands. They are the ones who make the decisions that affect you the most. Give them all the information they need to make good decisions.

Prices

There are two possible reasons why employees may demand more money when you share pricing information: either they deserve it, or they don't understand things like retained earnings, taxes, and return on investment. Don't hide the information. Share more of it so they understand how the business operates. Explain that top-line revenue is far different from bottom-line profit, walk through how one dollar of revenue flows through the business, and explain how the investors in the business need to receive a return on their investment. Explain how profit is used to fund expansion and growth. If they still have problems with the information, either they need more time to mature, or they have a personal compensation issue that should be addressed as a separate and distinct issue.

Bad News

The only thing worse than someone who is always negative and pessimistic is someone who is always deliriously happy.

There are always good and bad times. As a naturally paranoid manager, someone who always gives a rosy status report is probably one of the things that worries you the most. Sharing only the good news with employees lowers your own credibility in the same way. Besides, it's better to have as many minds as possible thinking about a problem and its solution. Don't forget, the issue is never just the bad news—the issue is how soon people hear about the problem. People can always deal with problems when they have enough time to do something about them.

Gary Van Dyke knows this first hand. By 1995, Van Dyke & Associates, a systems integration firm located in Bethesda, Maryland, had been in business for almost 20 years and had built a loyal base of employees, customers, and partners. Much of the firm's revenue came from partnerships with companies like Computer Sciences Corporation (CSC) and Booz, Allen & Hamilton. Early in 1995, Gary and his leadership team decided to take the firm out on its own and actually compete against the likes of CSC and Booz, Allen for three large federal government contracts. Winning the business would virtually guarantee growth for the next three years. Losing the business would mean just the opposite, or worse.

The good news is that Gary and his team put together a great proposal, and they involved a wide range of the people in the organization in doing so. Everyone understood the risks and potential rewards of going after those contracts directly. The rewards included growth and opportunity. The risks definitely included jeopardizing the company's future health by breaking off relationships with long-term partners.

The bad news is that Van Dyke & Associates lost all three contracts on one fateful day in July. They faced the challenge of replacing 25 percent of their revenue stream. They also faced the real possibility that employees who had seen a quarter of their future opportunities disappear overnight would panic and jump ship.

But the Van Dyke employees had been fully aware of the possibility of failure, and they rallied around the cause instead of jumping ship. By November, Van Dyke had fully recovered. Although revenue growth was relatively flat in 1995, the company actually became stronger. They overcame a great obstacle as a team, and lost only one person as a direct result of this event.

Share the good news and the bad news as soon as you get it. Your people will respect you for it, and it will raise your credibility. Most likely everyone will chip in to help; they won't run away.

Financial Information

What's the real purpose of income statements and balance sheets? To provide a comprehensive picture of the status, progress, and health of the organization? No. Read on.

You miss a golden opportunity to educate your staff if you regard the income statement and balance sheet merely as scorecards. We do not dispute the usefulness of financial statements as scorecards, but this is a passive and reactive use for them. We suggest that you also use them proactively as tools to educate the staff on how the company makes money, on the cost structure of the business, and on how revenue and expenses translate into profit. By doing this, you create businesspeople. And who better to work for your company than solid businesspeople?

Routinely share the income statement and balance sheet with your employees, even if your company is privately held. Teach your employees what the financial statements mean and how they interrelate. They will be pleasantly surprised, and they will make better business decisions because of it. They will also ask you a lot of tough questions, like why administrative costs are so high, or what goes into the bonus numbers. Be prepared to give simple, complete, and honest answers. If you treat every question respectfully, seriously, and honestly your credibility will

skyrocket, and your employees will become more productive.

Employee Feedback

Providing feedback on employees' performance is another
important aspect of information sharing. Effective feedback
is constructive and timely. This means that you provide
employees with information that enables them to understand what they did right or wrong, and you provide that
information immediately after you observe a positive or
negative activity. It also means that you avoid the traditional annual review.

Annual reviews were effective when employees did one
task, did it all year, and did it every year. Today, jobs change
all the time. Employees are involved in all aspects of delivering a product or service to the customer. Their jobs are
more complex because they are responsible for a *business
process*, not just a simple task. They need constant feedback,
coaching, and mentoring. The annual review is not sufficient, and it doesn't help you build trusting relationships
with employees.

The notion of taking notes on someone's performance over
an entire year and then springing an evaluation on them over
lunch is just silly. Not only are employees offended by this
tactic, a year can be a lifetime in today's business environment. You need to ensure that your employees constantly
improve at what they do.

You must constantly communicate with employees when
building an ownership culture. You must teach them about
the business and the customer. You must give them immediate and constructive feedback so they constantly improve
their ability to execute the company's operating model.

Successful franchise operations such as McDonald's excel
because they ensure that every franchisee operates the operating model better than even Ray Kroc, the founder of the
franchise, could. This can only be achieved through close
and continuous interaction.

Provide constructive, valuable feedback any time you notice a particularly positive or negative action, and meet with every employee under your supervision at least quarterly. Help your employees become better workers and better businesspeople. Discuss their accomplishments over the past three months, establish some goals for the coming three months, and identify a few things they should continue doing, start doing, or stop doing. Use the quarterly meeting as an opportunity to get to know each other.

Communicate the good news and the bad news. Reaffirm that you are partners in the success of the business and the success of each other. Learn from each other, and then get back to work serving the customer.

Trustworthy

Imagine an entire organization moving at the pace of change while acting as one. Imagine that managers are able to delegate a task or responsibility without hesitation; that employees are able to focus solely on a project, customer, or business activity with complete trust that those contributions will be recognized and fairly rewarded. Moreover, imagine an environment where managers don't have to delegate because their teams have already anticipated the need. Imagine that an employee can get a raise, bonus, or other reward just because a manager believes it is right, not just at the "appropriate" time. This is the essence of trust in business.

We refer to this kind of trust as a *blind pass.* Each colleague has the faith and trust that another will be at the right place at the right time to execute the right move. Everyone knows where everyone else is on the court.

Ownership culture is built on trust, and the only way to build trust is to be trustworthy first. Making and keeping commitments is essential to being viewed as trustworthy.

When you trust someone, you rely on their honesty, integrity, and character. Trust is built over time as you make and keep commitments. You have to make commitments, and you have to keep them. It is no good to avoid making commitments in order to avoid breaking them. That's a cop-out.

The first step is publicly committing to the tenets of an ownership culture. People need to hear that you are committed to teaching them about the business, that you are committed to rewarding them for their contributions to the success of the business, and that they are empowered to act on behalf of the organization. Make this commitment to everyone in the organization, and then never break it. This is the value proposition you offer your employees.

When employees ask sensitive questions about compensation, profits, costs, or prices, give them simple, honest, and straightforward answers. If they challenge you on specific elements of the operating model, or the cost structure of the business, view it as a sign of their interest and concern for the organization. And proactively offer information about the inner workings of the business whenever you get the chance. When the employees come to view you as trustworthy your ownership culture begins to take root, and trust becomes an important part of your culture.

EMPOWERMENT—A REPRISE

You engender trust and create the conditions for empowerment by faithfully following the actions prescribed by the TRUST mnemonic. The next step is to ensure that your business processes and organizational structure support and reinforce empowerment. You also need to manage empowered employees appropriately. Let's look at management first.

Never Let Them Fail

Employees must act on their own in order for empowerment to take hold and thrive. But the business owner or business unit manager is ultimately responsible for the business and therefore must have a measure of control. Balancing this dichotomy is more art than science, but establishing an effective communication and reporting structure is essential. Try this technique.

Always establish specific reporting guidelines with employees who have demonstrated the ability and maturity to act on their own. Let them know up front that managers are inherently paranoid. Whenever information stops flowing, managers begin to dream up all sorts of catastrophic situations. They think the lack of information means that something has gone wrong. Let them know that whenever you start to feel paranoid, you are going to send an e-mail or voice mail message asking for a specific piece of information. You may ask about costs, revenue, progress against a schedule, employee morale, or whatever else is nagging at you. Challenge them to initiate communication with you frequently enough so that they never get one of your messages. This is their indication that they are communicating enough, and this is your tool to ensure that you have the measure of control you need without interfering with empowerment.

Experienced and successful managers often run on autopilot. Intuition and gut feelings are as important as specific training and knowledge to successful managers. And it is very difficult to transfer intuition. Let your empowered employees know that whenever you get a flash of insight about how to deal with a particular problem or situation, you will share it with them. Establish up front that your goal is to educate, not to control. Give them the freedom to use your recommendations or to ignore them if they choose. But offer them anyway.

Your goal is to see that all newly empowered employees succeed. Whenever you delegate authority and responsibility to others, hold yourself accountable for their success. Don't allow them to fail. It demands a lot of your time, but in the long run it is the only way to ensure that empowerment permeates the entire organization. There is no better way to sow the seeds of empowerment than to point to the success stories of employees who have exercised initiative and been successful.

Enabling Empowerment

Ever have a customer tell you how off-base your ideas were—and known they were right? It's a humbling experience, but it can be extremely beneficial when you learn from it. Sometimes the best customers are the ones who let you know just how dumb you really are. Let's relive one of those embarrassing moments. It illustrates how important it is to design business processes and systems that enable empowerment.

Our first professional services business built custom computer systems. One of our major customers was a large organization with headquarters in Washington, D.C., and satellite facilities spread throughout the world. We were hired to build a computer system that would enable headquarters to monitor and control the activities of this widely dispersed organization. The satellite facilities were provided with a computer system to use for their day-to-day activities. All of the information generated by each facility during the course of the day could be packaged up and telecommunicated to headquarters. Headquarters staff could review the information and better direct the activities of the entire organization. The system promised truly impressive productivity gains.

We traveled around the world demonstrating the capabilities and promise of the system, and eventually we arrived at a facility operated by a notoriously hard-nosed and cantankerous manager. We knew we had our work cut out for us with this gentleman, so we had prepared ourselves. We gave a polished presentation and demonstrated the system's capabilities. Then it was his turn.

He said that he was impressed by the system's capabilities, and that he appreciated the importance of the information that the system would provide. Then the other shoe dropped. After about an hour and a half of diatribe, we got the message. Under no circumstances would this gentleman use a system that captured information locally and sent it one-way up the chain of command. He had been down that road before, and he wasn't going there again.

When the dust settled, and we had a chance to recover and think about his comments, we saw his point. This man had tremendous responsibility. He was called on to make important, critical decisions every day. And he was held accountable for the results—he was empowered. What he needed was a system to provide information to help *him* make the right decisions. He didn't need a system that helped someone thousands of miles away to monitor his work. That was the old model. If he was empowered to make the decisions and was responsible for the results, he needed information. If this system didn't provide that information, he wanted nothing to do with it.

We learned a valuable lesson the hard way that day. Any business process or system, automated or manual, that doesn't provide valuable information to the people responsible for making business decisions is a waste. It is not only ineffective, it works against empowerment in the organization. If people do not have the information to act appropriately, they do not believe in empowerment, and they do not act. Worse yet, if they don't have the information to act appropriately and they *do* act, what kind of results can you expect?

Does your financial system provide an accurate, timely, and complete picture of the company's financial health to all employees? Does your budgeting process enable people to learn from each other, or does their data just disappear into the accounting department, never to be seen again? Does everyone have access to example contracts, budgets, financial models, reports, and other artifacts, or are they kept under lock and key?

Information should flow down and around the organization, not up through the hierarchy. If individual empowered employees don't have access to information that is collected within the organization, question its worth. Your business processes and systems must provide accurate and timely information to the people who make the decisions. In an ownership culture, that means *everyone*.

An Empowering Organizational Structure

Small companies naturally avoid hierarchical management structures. The cost of several layers of management is prohibitive, so owners avoid them. Organizations that have few layers of management are known as *flat* organizations. Flat organizations are often synonymous with empowered organizations. The reason is simple.

The people doing the real work of the organization make the decisions if there are no managers. It's empowerment out of necessity. The challenge is to maintain empowerment as the organization grows and the need for management increases.

The traditional, hierarchical organization structure worked well in the past, but is losing its reason for being. Hierarchical structures were used to aid communication throughout the organization, but e-mail, voice mail, pagers, and the like have taken their place. And as most organizations now know, middle management adds to overhead costs and reduces the organization's ability to adapt to customer needs. An organization that fragments the decision-making process because of hierarchy is never as flexible as an organization that empowers the people closest to the customer.

As an organization grows, its sheer size and scope requires more management. How does the organization balance empowerment and hierarchy? What is the most effective organization structure for an empowered organization?

The goal of any organizational structure should be to push authority and accountability down to the people who serve the customer. That is where decisions must be made. The purpose of the organizational structure is similar to the role of business processes and systems that we discussed earlier. The organizational structure establishes roles that focus on increasing empowerment.

Management roles in the modern organization are communication roles. Managers are like sign posts throughout the organization. They are like highway information signs that give the location of the nearest gas station, restaurant, or hotel. When empowered employees need resources, guidance, or help, managers can point them in the right direction. This means that managers are not responsible for supervising people; instead, they must constantly stay on top of what is going on across the organization. This is in stark contrast to the traditional view that managers focus only on their own slice of the business—their project, business unit, or department. Today, managers need a broad focus across the organization. They need to know where the resources are and how best to allocate them across the organization. Then they must relay this information to the people closest to the customer. When someone has an issue or a need, it is the manager's job to point them in the right direction and to marshal the resources they need.

CTX Corporation is a rapidly growing, entrepreneurial company with an eye toward the future. As a growing business bent on taking advantage of its market and the strength of its workforce, CTX struggled with how it should organize itself. The company had a typical structure to begin with. It went something like vice president, director, project manager, worker. So we asked them what a vice president does. Well, vice presidents manage directors. So we asked them what a director does. They said, a director manages project managers. When we started to ask about the role of a director, the room filled with laughter. They began to see how the organization's structure didn't really support its business. It had been adopted because it was familiar and it provided a career path. Today, the company has adopted a more streamlined structure. Instead of vice presidents, they have internal franchise leaders (we wept with pride). Then they have team leaders. Finally, they have colleagues. The entire company is focused on executing its operating model in teams. *That's* an empowered organization.

Avoid the semantic battle over the definition of a flat organization. The real issue is whether employees are empowered, and whether the organization's structure helps increase empowerment. The number of managers or management layers is inconsequential. Many organizations have removed middle management layers through layoffs. But there's a big difference between a flat, empowered organization and one that has been gutted by reengineering and downsizing.

To determine whether you have a flat and empowered organization, always return to the fundamental conditions of empowerment. If your employees can go home at night, look in the mirror, and honestly believe that they are empowered to act, that they have the information and knowledge to act appropriately, and that they have the unconditional support of the organization behind them, you have an empowered organization. When you have the sense that you live and die by the actions and decisions of your employees, you have an empowered organization. After that, the number of management layers is unimportant. Focus on building the structure, processes, and systems that encourage and support empowerment.

CONCLUSION

An ownership culture is a corporate culture based on trust. All it takes is a commitment by management to teach everyone about the business, to reward employees when the business succeeds, to unconditionally support them, to share all information openly and honestly, and to always be trustworthy. Just remember the acronym *TRUST.*

Trust is possible in business today. Although it may seem unusual, it's not unnatural. People want to trust each other. If you create the right environment, trust can flourish, even in the high-stakes business world.

Not long ago, we attended the opening of options trading on the floor of the Chicago Board Options Exchange (CBOE). When the opening bell rang, more than 200 people gathered in a small pit began a ritual chorus of screams, shouts, and hand signals. They traded millions of dollars in options in this chaos. Nobody signed a contract. No committees were formed to decide on the trade. The traders simply shouted across the room and executed a series of intricate hand signals. Agreed-upon trades were jotted down on small slips of paper and placed on the floor. Runners came by, picked them up, and took them to technicians at various stations around the room, who entered them into the computer system.

Incredibly, less than 1 percent of the trades made on the option floor are rejected down the line. In other words, the system is nearly flawless. Very few trades are disputed when the time comes to close the deal and actually swap stock certificates or cash. This system is based solely on the word of the traders involved in the transaction. This is the world of high finance, and it is a truly trusting environment. Moreover, the system is self-policing.

Imagine that you are a trader in the pit, and you have just signaled the acceptance of a deal. Perhaps you agreed to buy a *put* option. A put is the right to sell a security at a set price. It is often used as a risk mitigation strategy when a trader believes a stock price is about to fall. If the market suddenly moved against you, and the stock price began to rise, imagine how easy it would be to deny ever making the trade. After all, several hundred people stood screaming around you, and in that environment, it would be easy to make a mistake.

You might get away with this tactic once. However, the next day you would likely find it difficult to get anyone to trade with you. The word would be out. You couldn't be trusted. Your career as a trader would be over.

Trust is possible in business. It's not the seeds, it's the soil. Your employees are okay. Focus on the environment. Focus on creating an ownership culture by performing the actions prescribed in the TRUST mnemonic. Cultivate your corporate soil and be prepared for an abundant harvest.

6

The Reward
of Ownership

Most employees have a fierce need to understand the rules of engagement within their organization. They want to know how they will be measured and how they can succeed. If the measurement criteria are not known, employees instinctively watch to learn how other people are rewarded and then strive to emulate the behaviors that they believe produce the most rewards. If you don't explicitly identify the behaviors you desire, employees make them up as they go along. It's much better to define the rules than to leave them to chance.

Compensation and incentive programs are the most important tools you can use to reinforce behaviors that are consistent with an ownership culture. Using these tools effectively depends on designing a reward system that is consistent with an ownership culture, ensuring that the rules of the game are widely known and understood, and never, ever, compromising. In other words, an effective reward system is appropriate, clear, and consistent.

APPROPRIATE REWARDS

An appropriate reward system motivates behavior that is consistent with high levels of initiative, accountability, team spirit, and external focus. Therefore, compensation and incentive programs must reward and motivate everyone to exercise high levels of initiative, to be accountable for results, to be a team player, and to focus on the customer. Employees should make more money and have more opportunities when they exhibit the qualities of a business owner. They should not be rewarded when they do not.

CLEAR REWARDS

All too often, a company's reward system is its best-kept secret. For some reason, managers feel that they have to control employee aspirations. This tendency is usually a side effect of a *scarcity mentality*. In other words, managers believe that they have a limited amount of compensation to hand out, and if everyone strives to accomplish great things, they won't have enough compensation to go around. So, managers avoid letting everyone know how to accomplish great things.

A scarcity mentality is also a side effect of viewing the organization chart as a career path. If everyone understands the organization's "secrets to success," too many people get promoted and the organization risks becoming top-heavy. The typical approach is then to make the criteria for promotion harder to achieve, so that the promotion rate declines. But the real effect is that the high achievers leave the organization to find better opportunities elsewhere.

A scarcity mentality is inappropriate in an ownership culture. It may have made sense when employee compensation was unrelated to company performance, but it no longer does when a direct relationship exists between employee actions, compensation, and business success. Managers can develop an abundance mentality, a belief that there is enough to go around for everyone.

Remember, in an ownership culture employees make decisions that materially affect the business. Therefore, it follows that the business will be successful if they make good decisions. Following this line of thinking, there should be more benefits to share with the employees when the business succeeds. The compensation system is self-funded by the actions of the employees.

In this environment, it makes sense to explain the rules of the game. Your employees will never completely trust that they are being compensated fairly if the rules of the game aren't explicitly understood. That's human nature.

We are not advocating that you publish a set pay scale. We are advocating that you identify and constantly emphasize the behaviors, skills, and attitudes that you value and that will produce personal and business success. Employees must understand that the company will reward these behaviors— and *only* these behaviors. If you value team spirit, you need to reward those who provide a helping hand. If you value customer focus, you need to reward those who go the extra mile for the customer. If you loathe politics, you must ensure that your reward systems fight political maneuvering.

The interesting thing is that employees don't spend a lot of time thinking about the rules of the game when you make them clear. They would rather focus on making themselves successful. And in today's business climate, that means focusing on the customer.

On the other hand, unclear rules cause recreational complaining—employees gather to commiserate about unfair compensation and all the other evils that the company commits. This springs from the unknown. People divert precious energy stewing about what they don't understand.

Clarity also fosters open communication. When everyone knows the rules, employees feel better about openly discussing compensation issues with management. They raise concerns and issues before looking outside the company for new opportunities. They feel that they can make an effective argument for more money or other opportunities. And, as long as you listen, honestly consider their viewpoint, and provide a rational counterargument if necessary, they will be satisfied. Of course, if they really are underpaid, do something about it. If you don't, somebody else will.

If you honestly determine that your employees are already fairly compensated, don't rebuff their requests for more money. Offer them concrete, specific advice on what they need to do in order to earn the additional compensation. Just make sure the objectives are tied to company performance. You both benefit if they achieve the new objectives.

CONSISTENT REWARDS

Consistency is where the rubber meets the road. Imagine that one of your top performers has violated one of the principles or values of your ownership culture. What do you do?

The answer is easy when it involves a below-average performer. But, what about that one guy you depend on? Perhaps everyone views him as being one of the leaders of the organization. He may have a loyal following within the organization. People look up to him.

Yet, he has a habit of not being a team player. He refuses to help his peers, for example. On several occasions, he has achieved his own goals at the expense of others. He has the habit of raising himself up by putting others down. But he gets business results. Now, what do you do?

Your answer had better be that you put an end to this behavior. You must immediately counsel this individual and, if his behavior does not change, you must alter his personal and professional rewards and opportunities. You may even have to ask him to pursue his goals elsewhere. You can't let top performers get away with breaking principles and values any more than you can let a below-average performer get away with it. Consistency is critical. Otherwise, all the goodwill you establish by designing an effective reward system and communicating it to everyone is shot. In one fell swoop, you destroy your credibility. The message you send is that principles and values are secondary to business results.

If you truly believe that your principles and values create success, don't sell them out for anyone or anything. Consistency under fire is critical to building the belief within your organization that when the company succeeds, everyone succeeds, but only when everyone plays by the rules.

THE TOOLS OF THE TRADE

Compensation and reward systems involve much more than just salary. Bonus programs, health and dental benefits, vacation and holiday time off, sick leave, and equity ownership, as well as the intangible benefits of working in your business, are all important elements of your reward system. For our purposes here, we consider compensation from four perspectives:

- Salary
- Variable compensation
- Equity sharing
- Intangible compensation

We discuss how each of these components can help motivate entrepreneurial behaviors while meeting the diverse needs of your employees. Along the way we dispel some common misperceptions about how compensation systems work to motivate and reward employees.

Salary

Salary is the traditional form of compensation. People won't even consider working for you without a base salary. Even sales-oriented positions usually involve a minimum base salary. As a tool to motivate employees, however, the value of salary is limited. Our experience has shown that the real value of a competitive salary is in attracting employees, not in motivating or retaining them.

In the course of building our first professional services business, we hired almost 350 people over 4 years. They were highly skilled computer scientists and engineers who often had advanced engineering degrees. Needless to say, they were in demand.

If the national unemployment rate is 5 percent, the unemployment rate for people with these skills approaches 0. If you are skilled in information technology and want a job, you can get one. Recent estimates indicate that there are close to 300,000 computer-related jobs open around the country. It's a very competitive employment market. In fact, it's a seller's market. Information technology professionals can choose where they want to work.

Because our business was dependent on hiring *and* retaining top-notch people, we were concerned about keeping our compensation programs competitive. We routinely polled our employees to assess the competitiveness of our compensation programs. The feedback we received was insightful.

There were always a few people who had personal compensation issues. They were the ones who labeled our compensation programs as inadequate. However, the vast majority indicated that they were not staying with our company because of the money. They felt that our pay structure was pretty competitive. They also knew that they could go across the street to a competitor and easily get at least a 10 percent salary increase, but we never had trouble retaining people. Our employee turnover rate was well below 10 percent in an industry that averages 25 to 30 percent turnover every year.

The most important lesson we learned by polling our employees was that salary alone wasn't going to retain any of them. The other aspects of working at our company far outweighed salary alone.

Don't get us wrong—our people demanded a competitive salary. If they had been underpaid by industry standards, the story would have been much different. Most of the people we hired wanted to know they were competitively paid, based on their expertise and abilities. They also wanted their salary to be commensurate with the effort they put in on the job. Over long periods of time, people began to feel underpaid when they were constantly required to put in extra time to get the job done. But overall, money was not their primary motivation.

When you set your salary structure, be careful not to overdo it. Most people won't turn down a little extra something in their paycheck, but don't assume that money is their main motivation for working. If you do, it can backfire. You start to attract people who are trying to cash in on a competitive job market. They are the same people who leave in a year to get another large pay raise, regardless of how much they enjoy the job. Someone always offers to pay them a little bit more.

Your salary structure should be a defined component of your operating model. You should offer a competitive, attractive salary that fairly compensates people for their expertise and effort. Earl Nightingale, the famed radio broadcaster, said it best. He said your salary is determined by the demand for what you do, how well you do your job, and how easy it is to replace you. That's good advice to follow when you develop your salary structure. Compensate people for their expertise and skill, modified by the conditions of the marketplace. Go through this analysis as part of defining your operating model. Avoid relying on higher salaries to motivate or retain employees. Use the other elements of your compensation program instead.

There is one exception to this rule. We found that the junior people in our organization, those with one to five years of experience, were very concerned about salary. Young people entering the workforce are trying to get established. They need reliable transportation—preferably a red sports car. They want to buy a house. Eventually, they start a family. They want to brag about their 15 percent pay increases to their old college roommates. The need for cash dominates all their other concerns. That's why so many young people find it difficult to save for retirement, even though they know how important it is to start saving early.

Young people expect a significant pay raise each year. Their focus is on improving their standard of living. They do want opportunity for personal and professional growth—but they also want that cash. Take this into consideration when you design your salary structure. Younger, more junior people should have the opportunity for larger salary increases early in their careers.

As people mature in their careers, retirement savings, personal and professional growth, and entrepreneurial opportunities begin to play more important roles. Another 5 percent salary increase begins to have less of an impact, and you can't afford to give your most highly paid people 15 to 20 percent raises every year. Besides, the more senior people in your organization are likely to have a larger impact on the performance of the business. Therefore, more of their compensation should be tied to business performance.

Salary is the foundation of your compensation package, and it's definitely vital to your recruitment efforts. However, salary will not normally set you apart, and salary alone is not an effective way to motivate people. Most people view salary as the payment they receive for doing a job—payment for services rendered. They expect to be paid every month as long as they do the job satisfactorily. If you try to motivate them to do more by raising their salaries, it usually doesn't work. The higher salary eventually becomes an expected part of their compensation, not an additional incentive. Just try to reduce salaries when people don't achieve their goals. They'll revolt.

Once you have the workers you need on board, the other components of your compensation programs need to play a stronger role in motivation and retention. That's where variable compensation, equity sharing, and intangible compensation weigh in.

Variable Compensation

The goal of a variable compensation program is to provide additional compensation when employees accomplish specific objectives that build the value of the business. Unlike salary, variable compensation is not payment for doing one's job. Variable compensation involves something extra.

Variable compensation is paid when someone achieves significant personal and business objectives. As such, variable compensation offers a unique opportunity to motivate people to act like owners of the business—but only if you strictly tie the payment of this compensation to the performance of the business and the individual's contribution to the business. Otherwise, the extra compensation is regarded as salary and becomes an expected part of their annual compensation. It becomes an entitlement.

Consider a standard bonus program. The program may be designed to encourage individual employees to accomplish specific objectives, such as increased sales, customer satisfaction, or lower costs. Normally, the bonus is paid when an employee meets established performance objectives. But what if the business has a poor year even though the employee accomplishes the objectives? Should the employee still receive the bonus payment? If you think so, you are violating the law of the entrepreneur.

A bonus program must be tied to the performance of the business to truly motivate someone to act like an owner of the business. In this case, the bonus should be paid only if the business meets its objectives for the year, usually as measured by revenue and profit targets. Once that threshold is met, then you should consider individual performance when determining whether to pay the bonus.

When you don't tie the bonus to business performance, you send the message that individual performance takes precedence over business performance. That's a dangerous precedent to set. What if someone offers steep price discounts in order to make a sales quota? What if someone avoids the opportunity to help the company win a large new customer because doing so won't get them immediate credit? Are you motivating the correct behavior?

You have to avoid situations where people can get ahead even if the company doesn't. Otherwise, you are out of alignment. You leave the success of your business to chance. There's no direct correlation between the activities of your people and the objectives of your business. You may have an indirect connection in the form of processes, procedures, and policies that control what people can do, but it's easier to encourage behavior that is naturally aligned with the goals of the business. Individual success is then a side effect of business success, instead of business success being coincidental to the agendas of individual employees, constrained only by corporate policies. Don't leave the success of your business to chance.

Use bonus programs to teach people about their ability to impact the business. Whereas salary is payment for working *in* the business, a bonus is payment for working *on* the business. Offer incentives and rewards to people who devise better ways of serving customers or figure out ways to reduce costs. Reward people for attracting new customers and new employees to the business. Use your bonus program to teach people that everyone needs to be vigilant about identifying better ways of doing things. Teach them that salary is payment for effectively *executing* your operating model. Bonuses are paid when they *improve* your operating model.

Equity Sharing

Stock option programs and other equity-sharing techniques are becoming commonplace. When you offer to share equity in your company, it is even more important to motivate an ownership mentality. Every time you issue stock certificates or offer someone the option to buy stock, you dilute the position of every current stockholder. If your company has 1,000 shares outstanding and you are the sole owner of the company, then you own 1,000 shares in the business. If you turn around and offer 200 shares to other employees, then you own only 800 shares. If the market value of each share is $10, then you have effectively reduced your stake in the company from $10,000 to $8,000. Therefore, your decision to share equity should be based on your fundamental belief that sharing the ownership of the company will significantly increase the future value of the company. This formula applies to both the smallest startup companies and the largest corporations.

If you can't concretely identify how sharing equity will increase the value of your business, don't do it. You not only hurt yourself, you hurt the other stockholders in the business. Their positions are diluted as well. Every decision you make regarding equity sharing should be centered on increasing overall shareholder value within a reasonable time frame.

Think about your objectives when you establish an equity-sharing program. If you are simply trying to reward employees, consider a variable compensation plan instead. If your goal is to increase shareholder value, then set up the plan so that those people who materially contribute to the value of the company—by creating customers, reducing costs, or improving your operating model—can share in the ownership of the company they are helping to build. Tie their participation in the ownership of the company to the company's growing value and their contribution to that growth.

Equity is not a silver bullet. Don't feel that people will act like owners only if they *are* owners in the legal sense. This is not the case. Some people would rather not be bothered. And others won't act like owners even if they do own stock.

You don't create *owners* by giving people stock—you create *investors*. Think about the personal investments you may have in publicly traded companies. Do you feel any sort of accountability to help those companies perform? Sure, you *want* the companies to perform—you probably *demand* that they perform. But you probably don't feel accountable for the performance of the businesses. Most of us don't even feel obligated to buy the products and services of the companies we invest in.

Investors hold *management* accountable for business performance, not themselves. Imagine your employees acting like investors instead of owners. It's the worst possible situation. They would hold you responsible for the company's performance even while they abdicated their responsibility to help the company succeed.

Don't even think about offering equity to employees until you have created and nurtured an ownership culture. You need an environment that motivates an ownership mentality first. Reward people like owners only when they act like owners. Everyone will be better off for it.

This is not a diatribe against sharing equity. In fact, we encourage it. Those people who materially affect the value of your business should share in its success. But equity sharing is not without its problems.

The biggest mistake we see is that employees' expectations aren't controlled. Very few people instantly become rich just because they own a few hundred shares of company stock. They need to understand this up front. The Microsoft story occurs only a few times each century. Morale can suffer when the company hits rough times and employees watch the value of their stock drop precipitously. As a business owner or leader, you know there are good and bad times.

You also need to seriously think through the dilution equation. Dilution is important. The Securities and Exchange Commission recently approved new rules that require publicly traded companies to report their quarterly earnings in two ways. First, they have to report basic earnings, or total earnings divided by the number of shares outstanding. Second, they have to report diluted earnings. This means that they have to account for the number of options and other equity instruments, such as convertible preferred stock, that might be converted to shares in the near term. This way, investors truly understand how much dilution they are dealing with.

If you are the owner of a privately held company, you need to ask yourself these questions: What do I want to get out of my business? How much dilution am I willing to endure? Am I willing to reduce my holdings 10 percent? Or am I willing to reduce my holdings 50 percent, even if it means I no longer have a controlling interest in the business? What am I trying to accomplish by sharing equity? Am I going to grant stock, or am I going to require that employees purchase stock? How am I going to value the stock? What happens if someone quits when they own stock? What happens if I have to terminate someone who owns stock?

After you answer these questions, it is critical that you be completely open and honest with everyone in the organization about your intentions. You need to let people know that you have no intention of sharing more than 10 percent of the company, or whatever the percentage might be. They must understand the terms and conditions of stock ownership up front. They need to know how the stock will be valued as long as the company is privately held. And most important, they should know the total number of shares that are outstanding.

We'll be frank. Too many business owners today con their employees by granting them a few stock options or stock certificates.

Slick business owners allocate a tiny fraction of the total shares outstanding to their employees. For example, an employee may receive 100 shares of stock when there are 100,000 shares outstanding. The net result of this transaction is that the employee owns 0.1 percent of the company. Unless the business someday becomes worth millions, the employee really hasn't received anything. Yet, the owner avoids telling the employee how many shares are outstanding because of the perception that employees want stock options. Down the road, when the truth becomes known, how do you think the employee reacts?

Because you are interested in the long-term success of your business and you value your relationship with your employees, put all your cards on the table up front. That way everyone can make their own decisions on the value of sharing equity in the business. You might be surprised how many people say no thanks when they see the big picture.

Equity sharing really is the ultimate form of entrepreneurial compensation, and it can be a powerful tool if you really believe in the wisdom of synergy. When structured correctly and used within the context of an ownership culture, an equity-sharing program can be a tremendously effective way to motivate people and increase the value of your business while sharing the rewards of ownership. Used incorrectly, it can become the bane of your existence.

Intangible Compensation

Intangible compensation, or what we refer to as *psychic income*, is the most underrated form of compensation. The amount of psychic income your employees receive is the single biggest determinant of whether they will stay with your company and continue to dedicate themselves to your business goals.

Psychic income is the value your employees ascribe to the type of environment they work in, the people they work with, their opportunities for growth, the challenge of the job, their ability to have an impact on the business, and the recognition and support they get from the company. Don't underestimate its power. Your ability to motivate and retain the people you need depends on the psychic income they receive from their jobs.

We will say it again: Your people want to be part of something big. They want to work with people they like, admire, and respect. They want to feel appreciated, be recognized for their contributions, and be respected. They want challenging opportunities. They want to be able to voice their opinions on the direction of the business. They want to feel that they own part of the business—regardless of whether they legally own it. They put a lot of value on these intangible elements of their jobs.

Get your people involved in setting the direction of the business. Ask for their opinions. Publicly praise their efforts on behalf of the business. Look for ways to say thank you. Challenge them. Empower them. Give them the responsibility they want. Respect their talents and abilities. The value they assign to these practices is priceless.

People don't normally quit for a 10 percent salary increase when they truly feel fulfilled in their jobs. In fact, most people don't like to change jobs. They like to stay put. Your ownership culture offers them reasons to stay. Eventually, when the word gets out, an ownership culture also helps you recruit employees. People who want to work in an ownership culture call and offer their services.

Your employees are talented and in demand. They can choose where they want to work. And, they want to work for a winner. Your willingness to build an ownership culture indicates that you are playing to win. Sooner or later the champions of your industry will come knocking on your door.

Psychic income is your best tool to decrease employee turnover. When people value their position in your company, they stay on the job. When people feel fulfilled by their jobs, they stay focused on the objectives of the business.

CONCLUSION

Effective compensation and reward systems signal your unending commitment to an ownership culture. Words are not enough. When you reward people for actions that are consistent with an ownership culture, everyone knows that you really believe in it.

People behave according to the way they are measured. Make sure your compensation programs reward people for acting like owners. Use the salary component of your compensation program to attract the talent you need. Ensure that your salaries are competitive with the industry. If you are in a competitive industry that is struggling to find talented workers, consider offering above-average salaries to attract people. Remember that younger, more junior employees require larger salary increases each year. More senior and higher-paid workers should receive a larger share of their compensation from bonuses, stock options, and other variable compensation plans that are tied to the performance of the business.

Once you have people on board, use your variable compensation plans to motivate them to act like owners. Structure your bonus plans so that the business is the primary focus of everyone's activities. If you consider sharing equity in the business, offer it only to those people that you feel will materially impact the value of your business, unless your objectives are liquidity or the need for capital. And offer equity only when you feel prepared to put all your cards on the table.

With your salary and bonus plans in place, focus on increasing the psychic income your employees receive from their jobs by nurturing your ownership culture. This not only improves your business, it provides your most powerful recruiting and retention tool.

People want to make a difference, and when you give them that opportunity they repay you with loyalty, hard work, and creative responses to your business challenges.

7

The First Signs of Growth

Just as seedlings push through the ground, here are the initial signs that an ownership culture is taking root in your organization:

- Initiative
- Accountability
- Team spirit
- External focus

When you recognize that your employees exercise initiative, accept accountability, work together as a team, and focus on the customer you can rest assured that an ownership culture has sprouted. These are the first signs that the seeds you've planted have germinated.

Let's look at each of these growth signs in detail. We describe organizations where these growth signs are prevalent and organizations where they are missing. That way, you can recognize their presence in your organization. Along the way, we provide some techniques that you can use to nurture and reinforce these behaviors once they begin to appear.

INITIATIVE

Initiative falls into that category of hard to define but you know it when you see it. High-initiative environments buzz with energy. Individual employees take action whenever something needs immediate attention. In high-initiative environments, projects take place simultaneously. This is not to say that they are always well coordinated or aligned with the direction of the company, but the urge of the employees to be a part of something leads them to volunteer and share their valuable time.

Is initiative present in your organization? Here's a quick self test:

1. Do employees take action immediately when faced with nonroutine issues that require attention?

2. Is most of the staff committed to growing professionally, personally, and technically?

3. Does the staff feel that the leadership team is committed to a growth pattern that creates opportunities?

4. Does your organization normally discuss failures and look for ways to improve?

5. Does it seem that things are never finished?

6. Does the company spend more time discussing how to grow revenues than how to cut costs?

7. Do employees generally just make things happen and keep everyone informed on how they went?

The more times your answer is yes, the more initiative your organization shows. When your ownership culture is fully developed, you can answer yes to every question.

Most of us have experience with organizations that lack initiative. They are characterized by a feeling that the status quo is good enough. They emphasize the classical management activities of controlling and monitoring, rather than leading and motivating. Since organizations that lack initiative fear the unknown, they spurn change. Paralysis sets in because there is a certain comfort with the current state of affairs.

These organizations seem to rely on rules and procedures more than on common sense. They seem to drain the life out of everyone who works there. Initiative is associated with bootlickers and backstabbers, and peer pressure to comply with the way things are done is very strong. Low-initiative organizations have established no *reasons* for employees to exercise initiative, so employees develop a "why bother" attitude.

Identifying Initiative

In the book *Leadership Is an Art*, Max DePree discusses a concept he calls *roving leadership*.[1] This is the essence of initiative in an ownership culture. Roving leaders don't walk by something that needs to be done. Roving leaders take action when the conference room is in a shambles and clients are due any minute. They don't wait to be told—they see something that needs to be done, take the initiative, and complete the task because it is the right thing to do. Roving leaders are one of the first signs of growth in an ownership culture. Identify them, create a supportive environment for them, praise them publicly for their actions, and encourage their behavior at every level of the organization.

An increased commitment among employees to grow professionally, personally, and technically is another sign that initiative is on the rise. Whatever your industry, employees must be willing to grow, and the organization must support that willingness. Corporate support can take all kinds of angles, and it doesn't need to break the bank. If employees attend a seminar or workshop, ask them to present their findings at a brown-bag lunch colloquium or an after-hours brainstorming session. If employees take a weeklong certification program, give them a couple more days to come up with a minicertification that the company can administer to other interested parties. Create a win–win environment for the professional development of all employees. Make it beneficial to both the individual and the company when somebody improves their skills.

We spent a great deal of money in our business developing our employees' communication and leadership skills, as well as their technical skills. Since our firm was made up mainly of employees with technical backgrounds, it was critical for them to stay current with the technology. But, it was just as critical for us to develop communication and leadership skills.

A majority of our employees worked directly with customers, and a high percentage of them had office space at our customers' facilities. Their ability to communicate ideas and solutions was a vital factor for the success of the business. So we developed a customized client-handling and communications program with the aid of outside experts.

The program was specifically tailored to our corporate culture, a culture that encouraged employees to act on their own and then communicate the results. Our employees began to show more initiative. They felt that the company supported them, and our clients began to feel that their concerns would be immediately addressed by someone with the authority to act.

Because we stressed leadership, we developed a leadership model that encouraged action at every level. This model had the effect of creating next generation leaders who understood our operating model and were motivated to make it a success. As a side effect, it fostered a high-initiative environment that spread throughout the ranks of the company.

Levels of Initiative

Stephen Covey often talks about six levels of initiative in his speeches. You can trace employees' growth as they move up Covey's levels:

1. Waiting to be told
2. Asking what to do
3. Recommending solutions
4. Acting and reporting immediately
5. Acting and reporting occasionally
6. Acting on their own

In other words, low initiative is characterized as sitting around waiting to be told what to do. High initiative is acting on your own. Employees naturally move through this progression as their skills grow and as they are challenged to exercise higher levels of initiative.

In an ownership culture, the hierarchy extends one level. As the five entrepreneurial beliefs permeate your organization, the seventh level of initiative becomes acting like an owner. At this level, employees not only act on their own, they act in a way that furthers the vision of the business. Their actions center on executing and improving your operating model. They are ready to internally franchise your operating model and act like owners.

ACCOUNTABILITY

History books are filled with tales of great leaders who held themselves accountable to the principles and values they believed in. Today society has discounted the virtue of accountability. Why is it that few people seem to hold themselves accountable for their actions? Why don't we ever read about CEOs who forfeit their annual bonuses because their companies missed their numbers? We'll let the sociologists and pundits debate this, but our experience has shown that many people do hold themselves accountable for their actions, given the opportunity. It's just not considered newsworthy. It's newsworthy when the CEOs of Fortune 100 companies receive compensation packages that are out of line with their companies' long-term growth and profitability.

Cover Your Assets

Petty politics is one of the ugly yet easily recognizable attributes of an organization that lacks accountability. Each person expends a great deal of energy on self-preservation tactics. This begins to put the emphasis on blame rather than on results. Employees assess the level of blame associated with any failure and then pass it around like a hot potato until it sticks to someone else.

In 1994, one of our accountability centers (our name for our business units), won a project to develop a system for the Internal Revenue Service. Our firm was contracted to develop the software for a system that would match W2 information with corporate tax returns.

Early in the project, we decided to switch hardware platforms. The IRS delayed in ordering the new hardware, and it was unavailable when we needed it. We discussed the status of the new hardware at a meeting with IRS officials. Although the software was being written for the IRS's Albany, New York, facility, the Washington headquarters was funding it, and John, whose job it was to order the hardware, worked there. Although a rather pleasant fellow, he seemed a bit detached from the entire conversation.

When a senior IRS official asked why the hardware hadn't been ordered, there was a deafening silence. Moments later the senior IRS official asked, "Aren't you accountable for this, John?" Another long pause. Finally, John gathered himself and said, "What do you actually mean when you say . . . accountable?"

Many organizations don't even know what the word *accountability* means, much less practice the behaviors associated with it. Excuses become the norm in these companies. Finger-pointing is a way to evade the reach of the headhunting management group. Recreational complaining replaces positive communication. Being accountable for anything is the farthest thing from the employees' minds.

Answer these questions to determine if accountability is an integral part of your corporate principles and values:

1. Do employees take action and follow up on the results of assignments made during meetings?

2. Does the leadership take ownership for the shortcomings as well as the successes of the company?

3. Is there a lack of finger-pointing and petty politics when issues need resolving?

4. Do your compensation and reward systems reinforce the behaviors associated with accountability?

5. Do employees treat adversity as a learning opportunity and commit to moving forward with even greater wisdom?

An ownership culture creates and reinforces accountability. Employees not only hold themselves accountable, they begin to hold others accountable. The fact that blame and judgment are no longer driving forces is one of the great powers of an ownership culture. Performance becomes the measure, and continual improvements in performance are in everyone's best interest. Assessment and improvement replace blame and judgment. The organization as a whole learns and advances.

Companies with high accountability are committed to improvement. They have either established self-improvement processes or developed an open forum for employees to test theories of improved performance. The improvements become institutionalized as part of the corporate fabric.

Turn up the Accountability, Please

Some companies just seem to have it. Did their employees swallow some sort of accountability pill when they were hired? What are these companies doing to create an environment where everyone takes ownership of their actions?

Beyond creating the environment of trust discussed earlier, your leadership team can take four specific actions to help create additional accountability within your company:

1. *Overuse the word* accountability. Include it in all of your meetings. Define it as it applies to your company. Discuss accountability in your corporate newsletter. Refer to people as being accountable for their areas of responsibility. *Accountability* is a very powerful word, and the more employees begin to use it, the more they will understand its meaning.

2. *Rename your business units* accountability centers. This is especially true if the business unit is a profit and loss center. The leader in charge of the accountability center becomes accountable for everything that goes on in that area. This eliminates that dreaded question, "What do you mean when you say . . . accountable?"

3. *Develop a meeting model that assigns action items and holds people responsible for completing those items.* How many meetings have you attended where action items were taken, then events seemed to overwhelm the issue and nothing got done? Keep a log. When an action is completed, update the log. If the action is not completed, the entire team will have a record of who was accountable.

4. *Review your current job descriptions.* Job or position descriptions naturally tend to establish parameters that can limit what gets done. Rework descriptions to describe roles rather than specific tasks. Everyone in the company is responsible for making the company successful. Job descriptions can institutionalize the dreaded phrase, "It's not my job."

INTERMEZZO—IS INITIATIVE AND ACCOUNTABILITY ENOUGH?

It would seem that a company that has created a culture where employees show a great deal of initiative and hold themselves accountable for their actions is well on its way to success. This is partly true, but these organizations can be still more successful by understanding that even a high-initiative, high-accountability culture leaves a few holes unfilled. Let's take a look at a matrix that has initiative on the x axis and accountability on the y axis (see Figure 7.1).

Quadrant I

Companies with low initiative and low accountability (Quadrant I) simply exist. You can find them in mature markets or even in an institutional setting, like academia or the government. Sometimes they are large Fortune 500 companies whose time as a major player in their industry has come and gone, but they stay alive through strong channels of distribution, customer loyalty to a specific brand, or an overwhelming market share.

Employees in these organizations tend to think of work as a means to a paycheck. The fear of disrupting operations

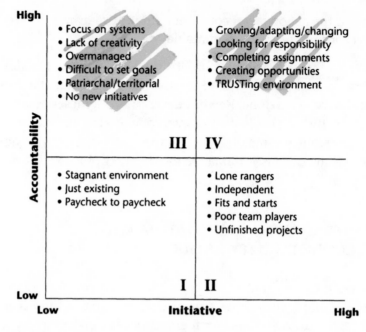

High
- Focus on systems
- Lack of creativity
- Overmanaged
- Difficult to set goals
- Patriarchal/territorial
- No new initiatives

- Growing/adapting/changing
- Looking for responsibility
- Completing assignments
- Creating opportunities
- TRUSTing environment

III | **IV**

- Stagnant environment
- Just existing
- Paycheck to paycheck

- Lone rangers
- Independent
- Fits and starts
- Poor team players
- Unfinished projects

I | **II**

Low

Low | Initiative | High

Accountability

Figure 7.1 Initiative and accountability matrix.

that have worked for 50 years is so strong, employees simply punch the clock, keep their heads down, and pick up their paychecks every 2 weeks.

Quadrant II

Companies that exhibit high initiative but low accountability (Quadrant II) radiate with energy and new ideas, but many projects go unfinished. They are characterized by fits and starts. A company that goes through an aggressive growth period, perhaps hires a large sales force, and then struggles to meet the new demand is an example. Employees begin to operate as lone rangers. They are very independent and don't see the need to work together. Compensation systems reward individual performance, but are generally not tied to corporate objectives.

Oracle Corporation was in Quadrant II in the early 1990s. Industry analysts agreed that Oracle's relational database product line was technically adequate but inferior to competing products from Sybase and Informix. To compete, Oracle became very aggressive in its marketing and sales approach. This was successful. Sales of Oracle's database products took off. However, its ability to produce quality products could not keep up. Also, sales representatives negotiated their own lucrative compensation packages, and would therefore try to sell anything that would add to their commissions. Their behavior was consistent with their measurements but was not in line with a sound long-term corporate strategy, much less the watchful eye of Wall Street.

After a rough period that saw a significant work force reduction, an acute stock price correction, and a dispute on how to recognize revenue in software transactions, Oracle has really turned around. The company still boasts a high-initiative environment, but it has also become accountable for the actions of its sales representatives and corporate officers. It has aligned its compensation packages with regional and market objectives. Revenue is recognized in accordance with standard accounting practices, and Wall Street continues to view Oracle as one of the software giants.

Quadrant III

Perhaps the majority of mature companies display low initiative and high accountability (Quadrant III). In these environments the focus is on systems. Things tend to be overmanaged and overcontrolled. Managers become very parochial and concerned about their territory. They spend their energy on bottom-line management instead of revenue creation. They look for ways to cut costs in order to give the impression that productivity is on the rise.

This problem is epidemic in second-stage growth businesses. As they continue to grow, they begin to focus on their bottom-line managers rather than their top-line leaders.

Bottom-line managers concentrate on the expense side of the income statement. They dutifully review each and every expense report to make sure it is in the operating budget. We've personally seen organizations that spend thousands of hours developing, reviewing, and reconciling operational budgets but spend very little time discussing their customers.

Top-line leaders focus on the revenue side of the equation. They understand that the only way to create new opportunities is to find new customers. Top-line leaders focus on substantially increasing revenues by finding new niches or expanding geographically. Top-line leaders build a leadership team that includes bottom-line managers, but the top-line leader is always first among equals.

Many growing companies experience an overwhelming urge to put a "manager" in place to control expenses. Obviously, expense control is important and essential to a company's long-term health, but revenue generation and the expansion of the top line should drive expense decisions. Stagnant businesses have an abundance of bottom-line managers. It is not a creative job. The hard part is top-line leadership. Entrepreneurial companies need to focus on revenue generation first and expense control second. Reward systems must reinforce the idea that profit results from revenue creation, not from simply slashing costs.

Quadrant IV

Companies that create a trusting environment create a culture of high initiative and high accountability (Quadrant IV). High initiative creates opportunities that are realized by highly accountable people. The organization continues to grow, leaders continue to make adaptive changes, and employees seek out responsibility. It's *almost* utopia.

Now we need to look for a couple of additional signs of growth, signs of team spirit and external focus.

TEAM SPIRIT

Initiative and accountability become localized over time, and companies must find ways for all elements of the company to become interdependent. Companies that consist of high-initiative, highly accountable business units still do not reach their potential, because units and individuals have not begun to rely on each other as a force multiplier.

That's where team spirit comes in. Individuals show signs of exercising initiative and accepting accountability. As they interact with other members of the organization, they form work groups. As the work groups become more sophisticated and they need to share ideas and solutions, they form teams. These teams take on a life of their own. Companies with no team spirit are filled with employees who don't understand how the vision of the organization relates to them. Employees don't consider corporate or business unit objectives as they make business decisions; they are motivated by the success of their individual actions. The vision of the leaders has not become operational.

A nonaligned reward system is typical of companies with low team spirit. Employees can meet corporate objectives more easily when they know what they are, why it is important to reach them, and what the positive and negative consequences of reaching them are. Employees remain independent when leaders leave team goals out of the equation. The real objective is to help them reach a state of interdependence.

The Help Model

The help model is an effective tool for developing team spirit. Use it as a force multiplier to expand your ability to serve your customers. The help model is a win–win–win arrangement. The company wins because it plugs holes in service and product offerings, employees win because they have the opportunity to expand their personal competencies, and the customers win because they are served by an organization whose whole is greater than the sum of its parts.

It is critical for the development of your organization that people seek help when problems that affect individual or business unit performance begin to manifest themselves. You have a very high probability of repeating the mistakes of the past when you don't ask for help. You can minimize the consequences of a bad situation by asking for and receiving help, and you can find alternative solutions to your problem.

Companies that have cracked the code of cooperation have a tremendous advantage. They go to market armed with the courage, competency, and intellectual capital of an entire workforce. Individuals can attack the most difficult problems, call the most difficult clients, and stretch their comfort zones with the full faith that the organization stands ready to assist them if things go wrong.

Our ability to work as a team was one of our biggest competitive advantages in business. We would normally have 3 to 10 people working on a particular customer assignment. But our customers routinely remarked that they felt as if they had a team of 100 supporting them. We zealously taught our people to rely on one another. We told them to seek help if they didn't know the answer to a question. We told them to find an expert in the company if they were stuck on a technical issue, and take the expert to the customer's site to fix the problem. We routinely looked for opportunities to introduce our customers to employees outside their core support teams. We wanted customers to know they had the full support of a 300-person company behind them, even if they were only paying for 3 or 4 engineers.

This process became an integral part of our operating model. Our voice mail system was probably one of the most productive tools we had. Our employees used it religiously to ask for help *and* to offer help. Our employees wanted to offer help, because doing so was acknowledged, appreciated, and rewarded. In fact, we often heard employees bemoan the fact that they were in a slump, struggling to find ways to help. Offering help became part of our culture and part of our operational focus.

Most companies have yet to figure out that asking for help is not a sign of weakness—it is actually a sign of intelligence. Problem solving is rarely best performed in a vacuum. It works best with input from a variety of sources—those with experience must chime in, and fresh ideas must be heard. Even those who say it can't be done have a voice (a *small* voice). The ultimate responsibility for the decision is not abdicated. It still lies in the hands of the person asking for help, but that person should feel compelled to search for other opinions.

Let's look at the help model in more detail. It consists of the following steps:

1. Anticipate the need
2. Ask for help
3. Become a servant leader
4. Show appreciation

Anticipate the Need

The first step in asking for help is anticipating your need. Make every attempt to understand your situation and anticipate your needs, and seek help before the issues turn into a crisis. Allow time for a response from those willing to help, and determine that what you ask help for is *important*, not just urgent. You can cry wolf only so many times before everyone ignores you.

Ask for Help

It doesn't make you less of a technician or a manager to seek out help—it makes you better. Think of the alternatives. You can select one of the most feasible options and hope that it is the right choice, or you can call a counterpart in another business unit who has faced something like this before.

The choice seems clear, yet asking for help is viewed as a weakness in most corporate cultures. This prehistoric position is most likely a holdover from a period in our industrial development when things just didn't change much. A manager who didn't know the production capability of a sheet metal extrusion furnace was considered incompetent. And perhaps rightfully so. However, times have changed. Everyone's job is more complicated today. More people are responsible for complete business processes rather than just tasks, and business processes are multidisciplinary. In this environment, is it fair to consider an employee who asks for help incompetent? The answer is no.

Create an environment that is conducive to asking for help. Your employees don't have all the answers. The most experienced managers don't have all the answers. No one person has the answer, but the opportunity for coming up with the right answer increases dramatically when an organization embraces the help model.

Employees must always feel that they can ask for help. Staff members can use communications tools such as e-mail, voice mail, teleconferencing, the corporate intranet, and the World Wide Web to seek help. Be clear and concise when asking for help. State exactly what you want. Make it as easy as possible for someone to help you. Explain the significance of the question and how the outcome will affect the project or corporate goals. Finally, if the request is for significant time, be prepared to build a short business case to support your request. A quick question regarding the air-travel system in Morocco is on a different scale than a request to travel there for a site inspection. Anticipate the scale of your need and be explicit in your request.

Become a Servant Leader

As the help model begins to work, your entire organization becomes sensitive to the concept that management encourages employees to ask for help. This quickly leads to the realization that the company must also encourage employees to provide help.

Servant leadership is an underlying theme in ownership culture. Robert Greenleaf, founder of the Center for Applied Ethics (now the Robert K. Greenleaf Center for Servant Leadership) and perhaps the world's best-known writer on the topic of servant leadership, felt that true leadership emerges from those whose primary motivation is a desire to help others. There must be evidence that this is true for the help model to be effective in any culture.

Becoming a servant leader means that you make serving others—employees, customers, and community—your top priority. In the help model, the servant leader is sensitive to the needs of others. Begin by putting yourself in the other person's shoes—make every effort to understand their need and what they are asking for. Here's an example.

Rick, a regional vice president of sales for Nabisco, knew that the opportunity to develop a better relationship with the headquarters team at Super Value (one of the nation's larger wholesalers) was critical to his personal success and was financially important to his company. Super Value was concerned that Nabisco was giving better deals to smaller regional wholesalers and was balking at moving forward in any new sales programs. Rick knew that other regional sales teams had great working relationships with Super Value's regional entities, and he set out to leverage his company's good name with Super Value's headquarters.

Rick lined up meetings and conference calls with various parties, fully intending to communicate Nabisco's commitment to Super Value's regional and headquarter operations. Other Nabisco regional vice presidents contributed their time to help Rick succeed. The result was a better working relationship with Super Value and an understanding among the regional sales groups that helping someone outside of their immediate areas of responsibility proved to be satisfying, rewarding, and profitable.

Servant leaders listen, have empathy, and try to make the situation more productive. At times this means responding immediately with an answer; other times it means pointing someone in the right direction. Sometimes persuasion is your most effective tool. Use every method of communication available to provide immediate relief and gain eventual insight.

You sense the development of community as your organization creates an awareness of the importance of serving. Division walls seem less impenetrable. Organizational boundaries don't keep people from serving and helping others in the organization. The sales group understands the issues facing manufacturing. Marketing understands that you can't promote products that aren't available yet. In short, employees begin to have an interest in serving the needs of others for the good of the entire organization.

Show Appreciation

The help model has three communication components. First, you ask for help. Then a colleague meets your needs. Finally—and perhaps most important—you *acknowledge* the help and *grow* from the experience. Failing in this final step makes the tool more difficult to use in the future. Not acknowledging the help makes you seem unappreciative. Failing to document the help and learn from your experience causes your colleagues to view you as lazy and incompetent.

When you show appreciation, make it public. A brief e-mail, voice mail, or handwritten note thanking the person who helped you goes a long way in perpetuating the model. A handshake in private sends a strong message. A handshake in the presence of the helper's supervisor supports and encourages an environment where serving others is a priority.

As you show appreciation, recognize that you needed help because you were weak in some area of expertise. Resolve to strengthen that area as part of your personal development plan.

The real strength of growing companies lies in their ability to create synergies between individuals within the business. Cooperative synergies direct skills and abilities to one unit with a weakness from another unit with a strength. The help model serves as the conduit for this type of synergy.

EXTERNAL FOCUS

You've created a culture of high initiative and high accountability. Disparate business units have begun to create synergies throughout your organization. Now it's time to make sure that your organization remains focused on the right target. An organization that shows the first three signs of growth will still not be productive if it directs its energy inward. It must have an external focus. Companies rarely go out of business because their internal processes are a mess. Companies go out of business when customers stop buying their products and services. If you stay focused on your customers, you eventually get a chance to fix your poorly functioning processes. The reverse is not always true. It may be too late to fix anything internally if you've neglected your customer base.

It is important that even the support elements of your business, such as accounting and human resources, have an external focus. We learned this the hard way. We had a subcontracting relationship with PRC, the billion-dollar subsidiary of Litton Corporation. This client represented about $3 million in business each year. Then our accounting departments began to squabble. PRC had directed us to provide monthly invoices for services rendered. But our accounting department had a better idea. They let PRC know that our company's policy was to do invoices twice a month. After accounting ignored a couple of requests for compliance PRC simply canceled the contract.

Our leadership team met with PRC senior managers on bended knee and with hat in hand. We wanted that 10 percent of our business back. We eventually rebuilt the relationship and the business continued to flow. However, the energy we spent on mending this fence could have been directed at new markets. We lost opportunities because the accounting department's focus was not in line with the customer's needs.

Develop an external focus throughout your organization as a way to live your vision. You never read a mission or vision statement that says, "We endeavor to have the best time-sheet process by the year 2000." Your mission is about your customers.

Companies with an external focus target new ventures, look for new markets, and expand their services to current customers. Companies with an internal focus build facilities to support the hierarchy within the company. Externally focused companies concentrate on increasing revenues. Internally focused companies concentrate on cutting costs. The more externally focused an organization is, the more in tune they are with the customer and market. Externally focused companies have built-in customer-focus teams. The teams know the market trends because they live in the market. They understand the needs of their customers because they spend a great deal of their time with them.

Chris Young, president of ProObject, illustrates this point perfectly. He reports that he is successful at finding new business because he is always around his customers. His competitor, on the other hand, sits at a desk at corporate headquarters. Chris often closes new opportunities before his competitor ever hears about them. That's the advantage of an external focus.

Here are two tests to help you assess your company's focus. First, spend the next two weeks taking loose notes on your conversations with your employees. Simply track the theme of each communication in your electronic calendar or in the back of your appointment book. At the end of the two weeks, tally the number of conversations that discussed internal issues, and the number that involved external issues. External issues include market trends, client needs and the competition, while internal issues are things like expense reports, budgets, facility issues, and accounting problems.

Review the results in terms of a customer attention ratio (CAR):

$$CAR = \frac{A}{B},$$

where A = number of externally focused conversations,
         B = number of internally focused conversations.

For example, if you had 30 externally focused conversations and 10 internally focused conversations, your CAR is 3. This means you spend about three times as much energy on external issues as on internal issues. Only you know if this is good, given the stage of your corporate development, but 2 or 3 is pretty good.

Second, consider Gary Hamel and C. K. Prahalad's external focus quotient (EFQ). They discuss the importance of looking externally, looking externally and forward, and, finally, looking externally and forward together in their book *Competing for the Future.*[2] The formula looks like this:

$$EFQ = A \times B \times C,$$

where A = percentage of time looking out,
        B = percentage of time looking out and forward,
        C = percentage of time looking out and forward together.

Think about the time you spend looking out. What percentage of your time do you spend focused on external matters like customers, competitors, or your next business opportunity? This represents A in the EFQ. For example, you might spend 30 percent of your time looking out.

Now, what percentage of that time do you spend looking out and forward? What percentage of the 30 percent of the time that you're focused on external issues do you spend thinking about what will be happening three, four, or even five years in the future, instead of just next week? Let's assume that you spend 30 percent of your external focus time looking forward. This represents B in the EFQ.

Finally, what percentage of the time you spend looking out and forward do you spend building consensus on the future? Do you spend this time alone, or do you engage your entire organization in a debate about the future? This percentage represents C in the EFQ. Let's assume it's 30 percent again.

To determine your EFQ, multiply the three percentages together. In our case,

$$A \times B \times C = 0.30 \times 0.30 \times 0.30 = 0.027.$$

In other words, you spend just under 3 percent of your time building consensus about the future of your company and your industry.

Hamel and Prahalad discovered that many corporate leaders score less than 1 percent. Leaders with a real desire to stay ahead of customer and market changes score much better than 3 percent. Use these tests regularly to assess your external focus.

PUTTING IT ALL TOGETHER

When your ownership culture takes root your employees exercise initiative in creating value for your customers and profit for your business. They accept accountability for their actions. They support each other and leverage your organization's total capabilities when serving your customers. And they remain focused on the customer, not on internal politics. The first signs that your ownership culture is working are initiative, accountability, team spirit, and external focus. It's critical that you have all four present in your organization.

Initiative without accountability results in a lot of activity but not a lot of responsibility. People may act, but they don't take responsibility for their actions. When initiative and accountability work together, people act and accept responsibility, but they act alone. They have a narrow, parochial view of their role.

When initiative, accountability, and team spirit work together, things begin to click. Your entire organization works together as a team. People act, take responsibility for their actions, and help others become successful as well. They understand that the success of the company is most important. They understand what's good for the franchise system is good for the franchisee.

Finally, when you add external focus to the mix, you have an explosive formula for business success. Your employee team is focused on serving the customer, together. They accept accountability for making your customers happy.

They work together to identify new opportunities. They stay focused on the future and your vision for the business. Their goal is to be the best that they can be, together. Your ownership culture has begun to sprout.

Like any good farmer, when your seedlings sprout you weed and feed. In an ownership culture, weeding and feeding means *leadership*—the subject of our next chapter.

8

Weed and Feed

In their book *The Leadership Challenge*, James Kouzes and Barry Posner identified practices common to successful leaders.[1] They found that successful leaders exhibit the following five practices:

1. *They challenge the process.* Successful leaders are pioneers. They challenge the status quo and look for new ways of doing things.

2. *They inspire a shared vision.* Successful leaders enable others to see the possibilities that the future can provide.

3. *They enable others to act.* Successful leaders enlist the support and assistance of all those who must make the project, process, or task work.

4. *They model the way.* Successful leaders are clear about their beliefs, develop detailed plans, and act as role models.

5. *They encourage the heart.* Successful leaders encourage their followers to carry on even though the climb to the top is arduous and long.

We believe it is critical that all leaders in an ownership culture embrace these practices. Here's why.

You ask employees to exercise initiative in creating value for your customers and profit for your business. You expect them to learn your operating model, to make effective business decisions, to accept accountability for results, and to stay focused on business performance. You are asking a lot, and are trying to accomplish extraordinary goals. It won't happen without strong leadership.

The five leadership practices identified by Kouzes and Posner are a perfect description of the strong leader working in an ownership culture. The good news is that these practices are observable and learnable. There is nothing mystical about leadership. Anybody can decipher the leadership code by embracing these practices and incorporating them into their daily activities.

Here's another simple mnemonic for actions that define effective leadership in an ownership culture. The mnemonic is COACH:

- Communicate
- Oversee team development
- Align business constructs
- Create next-generation leaders
- Create a Higher purpose

Most of us can relate to the concept of coaching. Good coaches instruct and demonstrate. They have a good understanding of how the game is played and how best to compete and win. Good coaches have excellent communication skills. They can motivate and inspire us in one-on-one sessions or in large group settings. Good coaches help orchestrate our actions and movements. They are intimately familiar with the dynamics of groups and teams and the necessity of working together. Finally, good coaches establish goals and inspire us to achieve them.

They set the bar just high enough to get that little extra out of us.

Let's consider the components of the COACH mnemonic.

COMMUNICATE

Effective communication is at the core of ownership culture and at the heart of good leadership. Effective communication enhances relationships, opens up possibilities, and encourages effective action. It's not about directing activities, tasking individuals, or gathering status. Good leaders constantly communicate messages about the customer, the company, and the future.

Monitor your discussions with employees. If employees are focusing on small, tactical issues, ensure that you discuss the big picture more often. If they are rejecting more responsibility and authority, make sure you discuss how the business works. Their lack of initiative may be the result of a lack of confidence or knowledge. If they are stuck on the status quo, discuss the opportunity that change provides.

To change someone's behavior, you need to alter their perception of what is possible and appropriate. Then their attitudes begin to change, and eventually their behavior changes as well. It all starts with communication.

Let's look at two important aspects of communication: sharing knowledge and using communication tools.

Sharing Knowledge

Sharing knowledge can profoundly impact virtually every organization. In its simplest form, sharing knowledge is simply making use of work you've done in the past. We all use knowledge when we avoid making the same mistakes over and over. When we pass those experiences on to others, we share our knowledge.

The feeling of individual satisfaction when you solve a specific client problem after months of effort can be exhilarating. However, if you never share the knowledge you gained through that trial and effort, someone in the organization will undoubtedly repeat the same mistakes. You have to make use of your corporate knowledge.

Using Communication Tools

Leaders who use voice mail, e-mail, online forums and communities, and a host of other technologies can dramatically increase the reach and effectiveness of their messages. However, technology is not a panacea. You need a broad range of communication tools.

Here is a list of tools to help you communicate more effectively.

1. *Eye-to-eye contact.*   Never lose site of the fact that the best way to build trusting relationships is through one-on-one communication. No matter how effective you become with technology, always keep good old-fashioned, eye-to-eye conversation in your toolbox. Nothing is more effective than looking someone in the eye, shaking their hand, and directly telling them your vision for the future.

2. *Team meetings.*   Use meetings effectively. Don't get a group of people together to read you status reports. Use written reports, e-mail messages, or voice mail for that. Use meetings to brainstorm new ideas, share lessons learned, and build relationships. Set the goal that every meeting should result in a breakthrough on an important business issue.

3. *Community forums.*   Create events such as community forums for your entire organization. They can be held monthly, quarterly, or annually depending on the size of your organization. Turn them into revival meetings. Don't drone on about operational issues—build excitement about the company and the future, reaffirm your vision and purpose, and celebrate accomplishments. Get people together outside of the daily grind, so they can build new relationships.

4. *Listening.* A great communicator is also a great listener. You must be able to read your audience and sense the mood of the organization. You can deliver a terrific stump speech, but if you're not in tune with your audience, your eloquent message falls on deaf ears. A great communicator delivers a timely message only after keenly observing the audience.

5. *Voice mail.* Voice mail is great for communicating messages about operational and tactical issues. You can ask for project status, receive updates on customer problems, and just keep in touch with the pulse of the organization. You schedule fewer meetings when you use voice mail this way.

Use voice mail to share knowledge as well. This was one of our secret weapons in our technical services business. Our consultants routinely sent voice mail messages to the entire staff when they were having difficulty with a particular technology or product. Other employees would respond to the messages and offer advice, counsel, and insight. The positive effect this practice had on our business is incalculable.

6. *E-mail.* Each week Bill Shrader, CEO of PSINet, crafts a one-page message and sends it to his entire workforce. This message usually relates an industry announcement or event to PSINet's vision and corporate objectives. Bill uses e-mail to inspire a shared vision among his employees.

7. *Virtual communities.* The best way to share information is to put it in a place where people gather. Virtual communities, like the Motley Fool message boards on the Internet (www.fool.com), are great examples of online forums for sharing information and keeping everyone informed. These forums are the online equivalent of the coffee house, barber shop, or workers' pub—a place people go to get the word on what's going on.

8. *Newsletters.* Use your newsletter as a marketing tool. Think of it as a tool to build relationships throughout the organization and promote the unique culture of your company. Use the medium that is right for your company. Ideally, you should e-mail it to every employee with the full expectation that it will float around in the industry for a couple weeks. Some companies naively feel that their newsletter information is confidential. Nothing could be further from the truth. Think of your newsletter as a promotional opportunity and a marketing tool in branding your ownership culture.

Use all the tools at your disposal to stay in regular contact with your employees. Communicate, communicate, communicate, and then communicate some more.

Oversee Team Development

What do leaders do every day? They build teams—teams that function on their own without a lot of direction or support. The question is, how do leaders build self-managed teams? Management guru Ken Blanchard came up with a great answer.

Blanchard developed the situational leadership model as a framework for understanding how leadership actions affect team performance.[2] He defined four stages in team development:

1. *Orientation.* The morale on the team may be high, but productivity is lacking. The team is new and excited about the task, but is completely unproductive.

2. *Dissatisfaction.* Until productivity begins to pick up, morale may decline. Team members become dissatisfied with their progress and conflicts arise.

3. *Resolution.* When productivity finally begins to pick up, morale begins to increase again.

4. *Production.* The team begins to act on its own and record impressive results.

Because all teams progress through these stages, a good leader must recognize the current stage of the team and then act appropriately.

When your team is in the orientation stage, you should direct people's activities in order to clarify roles and develop skills. Direction still applies in the dissatisfactions stage, but you also need to support the team and resolve conflicts. When your team enters the resolution stage, you truly become a coach. Your job is to support people as they grow in accountability and responsibility. Finally, when your team enters the production stage, you get out of the way. You let the team act on its own and simply monitor its performance against goals.

Learning to delegate is one of the most difficult aspects of leadership. Inexperienced leaders often struggle to let go of responsibility and authority. They feel exposed when they aren't in the middle of every decision, they don't know when to get involved and when to stay away, and they often rely on only one leadership style.

The situational leadership model helps you delegate more effectively. It teaches you that all teams evolve. Therefore, your leadership style must evolve as well. When you master this approach, your teams perform better, contributing to the presence of an ownership culture. Teams become the locus of control within the organization, and decisions are therefore made closer to the customer. Team members feel more productive and accountable. They make more decisions on their own, and they act appropriately, with the best interests of the business at heart, because you have taught them the business.

Align Business Constructs

Every business depends on effective processes, procedures, policies, and systems to operate efficiently and effectively. These are the *constructs* of a business. Unfortunately, too many organizations let their business constructs drive the company. This tendency manifests itself in thick policy manuals, inflexible procedures, and, eventually, disgusted customers.

As a leader, your job is to ensure that your business constructs align with your business focus and your ownership culture. Every new policy or procedure that you institute either supports and enhances your vision for the business or detracts from it.

Let's assume that you want to hire only employees that fit well in your culture. Although a skill match is still important, you want to ensure that attitude is considered in the hiring process, as well. How well do your processes, procedures, and systems support this goal? Consider your recruiting process, your employee development process, and your reward systems from this perspective.

Ask yourself these questions: Does my recruiting process test for cultural fit? Do we even talk about culture during an employment interview? Does my orientation program explain our culture to new employees? Do employee training programs address nontechnical skills that are important in our organization? Does my reward system consider attitude, or is it based solely on technical performance?

Your recruiting process screens for cultural fit if your constructs are aligned with your business vision. You offer training programs that address important nontechnical skills, and your reward systems consider attitude as well as technical aptitude. Otherwise, your constructs aren't aligned. You may really want to hire employees that fit your culture, but your business constructs don't help you achieve that goal.

Test every new policy, procedure, or system you consider to determine whether it supports your business vision and your ownership culture. Here are a few handy filter questions to analyze new business constructs:

- Does the construct encourage and support empowerment?
- How does information flow in the new process? Does it flow down and around the organization, or does it flow up the hierarchy?
- What is the purpose of the new construct? Does it help us serve our customers, or does it serve the internal needs of the organization?
- Will the new construct build equity in our ownership culture?

Don't decide on new policies, procedures, and systems flippantly. Consider each one individually on its merits. Keep your constructs aligned.

Create Next-Generation Leaders

Are you an owner of your business or a steward of your business? You need to be both.

Ownership implies the legal right to the possession of something. *Stewardship* implies the management of another's property, finances, or other affairs. At first glance, these two terms seem to be diametrically opposed. But nothing is further from the truth. Ownership and stewardship together form the perfect balance of short-term and long-term perspectives.

Always act like an owner, but view yourself as a steward of the company, as well. You are in charge of keeping the company going for the future. You do that by creating next-generation leaders.

The most important leader in your organization is the next one. The only way to secure a business that is dependent on highly skilled, talented workers is to develop new leaders. Here's an example.

Assume for a minute that your company's revenue growth is directly related to the number of people in your organization. This is most likely the case if it is a service-oriented business. Answer the following questions:

- What is your projected revenue for the upcoming year?
- What is your targeted revenue per employee?
- What is your average team size?

As an example, let's consider Silicon Technical Services, a very typical (although fictitious) software services company. In 1998, their revenues were $45 million. Since they bill on a time and materials schedule (2,000 hours per year) and their average hourly billing rate is $90, their current revenue per employee is $180,000. Let's assume that their average team size is 5, and that every team is led by a team leader. This means that the number of team leaders required is as follows:

Team leaders

$$= \frac{\text{revenue}}{\text{revenue per employee per year} \times \text{team size}}$$

$$= \frac{\$45,000,000}{\$180,000 \times 5} = 50.$$

This suggests that Silicon Technical Services presently needs 50 team leaders to manage the work they perform during a year.

Now, let's assume that Silicon Technical Services sets a revenue target of $85 million for the year 2002. They also forecast that their average billing rate will increase from $90 to $100. This means that their revenue per employee will increase to $200,000. However, they expect their average team size to remain at 5.

Given this new scenario, the number of team leaders required in 2002 is as follows:

$$\text{Team leaders} = \frac{\$85,000,000}{\$200,000 \times 5} = 85.$$

In other words, Silicon Technical Services needs an additional 35 team leaders to address projected growth.

As these examples show, the development of new leadership talent is central to Silicon's success. Use the leadership math formula to quantify the number of leaders you need to develop. You'll discover that developing new leaders is one of your key responsibilities.

Create a Higher Purpose

Your higher purpose is about your company's reason for being. You must envision a future that your employees find compelling. Then you must constantly communicate your vision of that future. In short, you must make a declaration about the future.

The Stump Speech

Encourage each of your next-generation leaders to develop a stump speech containing their declaration for the future. They can use this speech to communicate the corporation's higher purpose to stakeholders, partners, customers, and prospective employees. Suggest a few simple rules to help them develop the speech:

- *Always respect the past.*   Respect the efforts and accomplishments of your predecessors, and don't dwell on past failures.
- *Speak frankly about the reality of the present.*   Nothing kills your credibility as a leader more quickly than misrepresenting how things currently work.
- *Develop an unbounded enthusiasm for the future.*   Envision a future that everyone can get excited about.

Have them develop the speech in the context of their understanding of how the business operates and how they fit into the business. Get them started with something like the following:

Today, I would like to describe the future I see for the Consumer Products Division of Sweet Tooth Confections, Inc. and the possibilities the future will provide for all of us. . . .

Each leader in the organization uses the stump speech to inspire every person in the company. Next-generation leaders use their speeches to align their division or market segment with the company's higher purpose.

The value of the stump speech comes from the effort it takes to create it, and the number of times it is repeated. Leaders must be able to unleash a version of the stump speech on a moment's notice. Create two or three versions. Be prepared to deliver one any time you're in front of more than one or two employees, any time you meet a customer or a prospective customer, and any time someone asks you what your company does.

A higher purpose makes you attractive to candidates, clients, prospects, and Wall Street. It makes it exciting to get up in the morning, makes you proud of what you do for a living, and helps you establish your legacy in the business world.

It's All about Leadership

You are likely inflicting serious change on your organization by choosing to embrace the principles and values of an ownership culture. Therefore, effective leadership is critical. You must lead the change.

John Kotter outlines an effective eight-step process you can use to introduce an ownership culture in his book *Leading Change*.[3] We offer it as another framework for understanding your leadership responsibilities.

Here are his eight steps, with some commentary on how each one applies to the challenge of creating an ownership culture.

1. *Establish a sense of urgency.*   Discuss the changing business landscape and the changing attitudes and expectations of today's employees. Build a case for change, citing the consequences of inaction.

2. *Create a guiding coalition.*   Nothing of substance is ever accomplished by just one person. It is critical to build consensus on the benefits of creating an ownership culture. Solicit help from colleagues, subordinates, and those in positions of power. Look for those who are influential in the current culture.

3. *Develop a vision and a strategy.*   Use the operating model framework introduced in Chapter 3 to communicate your vision of where your organization is going and how it will get there.

4. *Communicate the vision of change.*   Communicate the case for change to all employees. As a leader, recognize that you can never tire of communicating your visionary message. Use all your communication tools.

5. *Empower broad-based action.* Break down barriers that inhibit the growth of initiative, accountability, team spirit, and external focus. Reward those who take responsibility for improving business performance. Align your business constructs with your vision and strategy.

6. *Generate short-term wins.* Create a couple of sure-win scenarios. Generate some excitement. Publicly celebrate employees who work as teams and focus on the customer. Honor and reward those who embrace initiative and accountability.

7. *Consolidate gains and then change some more.* Sometimes too much change feels like trying to drink from a fire hose. Delicate balance is required. Stay connected to your workforce. Look for signs of stress. Be a good listener. Encourage the heart every step of the way.

8. *Institutionalize the change.* Update your stump speech to reflect the new change. Modify your business constructs as appropriate. Develop an internal marketing program that drives the change deep into the organization and makes it part of your culture—part of your brand identity.

It doesn't matter if you view leadership in terms of the five leadership practices identified by Kouzes and Posner, or as a process of managing change as prescribed by Kotter. An ownership culture is all about leadership. In fact, business success itself is all about leadership.

Peter Drucker said it best: The only things that happen naturally in an organization are confusion, friction, and malperformance. Everything else is the result of leadership.

9

The Harvest

Your harvest takes the form of improved business performance. It results from the daily activities of well-informed, motivated employees, and it manifests itself in improvements to your key management indicators (KMIs). Business performance improvement is found at the intersection of your KMIs and the signs of growth in an ownership culture.

Any leader-induced change, such as the creation of an ownership culture, must be specifically measured against your KMIs. A great deal has been written on management and leadership concepts over the last decade, and much of it has at least some degree of merit. However, many of these concepts have failed in the marketplace because of their lack of practicality. They lost momentum because they either were unnatural gimmicks or were unmeasurable.

An ownership culture is not only natural, it's measurable. As two guys in the computing industry, measurement is very important to us.

The process of measuring your organization never comes to an end. As soon as you're satisfied with one element of your business, other parts need attention. Just when you reach your goals for customer retention, you've overlooked your next generation of leaders. Just when your revenue improves, expenses wobble out of line. The cycle of evaluation, measurement, and change is continuous in an ownership culture. The failure to conduct such a review regimen leaves you open to incredible inefficiencies and missed opportunities.

The measurement cycle is simple, yet fundamental. First, measure your culture to determine if the signs of growth are present. Next, map the signs of growth to your KMIs to identify initiatives to improve your business performance. Let's look at both steps.

Measuring Your Culture

Is your organization filled with high-initiative, highly accountable people? Does your division or business unit exhibit a high degree of team spirit and external focus? You may not have definitive answers to questions like these, but it is critical that you at least develop a gut feeling for where your organization fits in the range of possibilities.

The accountability assessment shown in Figure 9.1 is a simple test to measure the signs of growth in an ownership culture.

Although this assessment wouldn't pass muster in the academic world, it serves a useful purpose. Simply add the number of odd-numbered questions that you answer *false* to the number of even-numbered questions that you answer *true*. The higher the score, the more confident you can be that accountability is alive and well in your organization.

We suggest that you develop similar tests for your organization. Make them specific to your workplace, and routinely check your organization for the existence of team spirit, external focus, initiative, and accountability.

A Quick Accountability Assessment of Your Organization

account-ability The ability to account for, especially one's acts; to take ownership for what is happening.

True or false—as I reflect upon my immediate organization, I believe:

1. Many people think their career development plan is driven largely by a supervisor.

2. Most people have a little too much on their plates.

3. Employees usually stay within their own project or job descriptions.

4. We take action and follow up on the results of assignments made during meetings.

5. We are not always given increased authority, resources, and encouragement when we are given increased responsibility.

6. The leadership takes ownership for the short-comings as well as the successes of the organization.

7. The way things are (people, processes, and structures) often gets in the way of real progress.

8. We know our principles and values and enforce them at all levels.

9. There is a fair amount of finger-pointing and blame when things go wrong.

10. When mistakes or failures occur, we think of them as tuition and teach everyone else what we have learned.

Figure 9.1 Accountability assessment.

11. Some of our compensation and reward systems do not reinforce the desired behaviors we need for success.

12. Most of us treat adversity as a learning opportunity and commit to moving forward with even greater wisdom.

Figure 9.1   *(Continued)*

There are very formal tools in the marketplace that test for ownership culture values similar to the ones we describe. Chris Mackin of Ownership Associates has developed one of the best surveys available. The Ownership Culture Survey is a formal corporate survey derived from research on large corporations that utilize employee stock option programs (ESOPs). The surveys provide insight on many of the attributes associated with an ownership culture, although they can be expensive to purchase, conduct, and evaluate.

Pay attention to the signs of growth in your organization. Measure their presence in your culture continually, and measure again as you make adaptive changes.

The process takes time. Not every organizational itch can be scratched overnight. The critical factor is that you continue to measure your current environment and then make adaptive changes. Here's an example how this measurement process can work.

ProObject is a software development and systems integration firm located on the outskirts of Washington, D.C. As the company grew in size and matured in outlook, it began to review its executive compensation system. The leaders of the business were unhappy with the existing system. It seemed that the compensation system motivated the executives to stay independent of each other. The leaders decided that the system was not having the positive effect they had hoped for, as it was not forcing the leadership team to work together.

ProObject's leaders embarked on an effort to better understand the behaviors they were trying to motivate. They studied and investigated new compensation programs, such as a targeted bonus program that was closely aligned with individual performance and the company's revenue and profit goals.

ProObject measured again after implementing the new program, and they saw a marked improvement. Team spirit was on the rise, and their adaptive change was working.

MAPPING THE SIGNS OF GROWTH

The performance improvement matrix measures the impact of the signs of growth on business performance. It identifies specific ways that employees can impact a specific KMI.

Consider a performance improvement matrix (see Figure 9.2) for a software product company that has identified the following KMIs:

- Revenue per employee
- Customer retention rate
- Sales backlog
- Profitability

The first question you ask is how an employee can improve the first KMI (revenue per employee) by exercising initiative. Your answers might include the following:

- Sales representatives take the initiative to call on existing clients more often, resulting in increased sales (sales backlog).
- Programmers proactively identify productivity improvement measures that reduce the amount of labor required to develop a new product (revenue per employee).

	Initiative	Accountability	Team spirit	External focus
Revenue per employee	Improve programmer productivity.			
Customer retention rate		Receptionist tracks customer calls.	R&D solves customer problem.	
Sales backlog	Increase sales to existing clients.			Customer service reps sell additional products.
Profitability	Lower production costs.	Lower costs by 10%.	Work together to ensure profitable bids.	

Figure 9.2 Performance improvement matrix.

- The manufacturing department proactively develops an online software distribution tool that lowers production costs involved with mailing diskettes and CDs to customers (profitability).

Repeat this process for the other three signs of growth, and fill in the cells of the matrix with specific employee behaviors that improve the KMI. Here are some examples:

1. Accountability

   - The receptionist accepts accountability for ensuring that every customer call is directed to an appropriate person, not to voice mail. Customer service and retention improve (customer retention rate).
   - Each department head commits to lowering expenses by 10 percent (profitability).

2. Team spirit

   - Employees from finance, engineering, and sales work together closely and submit a winning *and* profitable bid (profitability).
   - Employees in R&D accept accountability for customer problems and help the customer service team soothe a disgruntled customer (customer retention rate).

3. External focus

   - Customer service representatives look for opportunities to sell additional products or services when they interact with customers (sales backlog).
   - The sales team stays tuned to the marketplace and identifies significant new business opportunities that would have gone to a competitor (sales backlog).

The improvement opportunities are limitless. The goal is to find specific, tangible actions that employees can perform every day.

IT'S A LONG ROW TO HOE, SO GET SOME SHARP TOOLS

Every day, employees make decisions that dramatically impact your company's performance. A sales representative fails to return a call, and a customer fails to renew a maintenance contract. Poor customer service loses a customer forever.

You've done a lot of hard work. Don't let your initiatives die on the vine because they are misunderstood at the grassroots level.

That would be like a farmer working all spring and summer in the fields, only to wait too long to harvest and lose the crop to an early frost. Don't let this happen to you.

You need to devise simple metrics that drive home the main point: Employee actions directly impact business performance. Let's consider some examples.

One of the KMIs we use in our technical services businesses is average billing rate—the average price we charge a customer for an hour of services rendered. Our CFO joked during one KMI review that our average billing rate was actually lower than the rate we paid the clown who performed at our annual company picnic. That Bozo was charging more to paint children's faces than we were charging our customers for advanced software engineering services.

Our rates weren't bad, but they were below the market average. Our managers were so eager to win new business that they were pricing our services below market levels. The *clown rate* rallied our managers to increase our average billing rate. No one wanted to run a project below the clown rate. We simply asked our managers to ask for $1 more every time they bid a new project. From that point on, our average billing rate climbed, and so did our corporate profitability.

The point is that we found a tangible indicator we all could relate to—not some esoteric term like return on invested capital (ROIC) or economic value added (EVA).

Those terms work well on Wall Street, but they don't translate well to Main Street. We all need to find our clown rate.

Here's an example of a useful metric from Southwest Airlines. Southwest's team calculated the total profit per flight, then divided it by the average fare. They discovered that a flight becomes profitable when 75 customers board the plane. Moreover, they learned that only five customers per flight accounted for Southwest's total profit in 1994.

This simple metric communicates a powerful message. If every ticket taker, flight attendant, mechanic, and pilot understands that company profit comes from only 5 passengers per flight, they know that 1 unsatisfied customer can reduce the profit on any flight by 20 percent.

As another example, Bill Toler, president of Campbell Sales Company, teaches his salespeople that each sales call is critical. He calculates that each sales call costs Campbell $50. That means that every time a salesperson enters a grocery store, the company loses money unless they sell an incremental $50 in soup or other products.

The simpler the message, the more profound its impact.

Make It a Game

Beyond the Box Corporation developed the Risks and Rewards business simulation game, a customizable board game that simulates a company's operating model.

The game helps everyone in an organization create a line of sight between their daily activities and the performance of the business. It's a fun and effective way to show people that their actions have a direct impact on the business. Figure 9.3 shows a photograph of the game.

Employees who play the game experience real-life business transactions such as closing customer sales, paying business expenses, and collecting receivables. They implement business strategies, record transactions on an income statement, and learn how to use a balance sheet.

Figure 9.3 Risks and Rewards game. Used with permission of Beyond the Box Corporation.

Employees discover that their individual performance can determine whether a customer sale generates a profit or becomes a loss. They learn how important it is to support the organization's strategic initiatives. They learn about retained earnings, realize that business growth provides opportunity, and understand that the availability of cash affects decision making.

Every transaction is a real-life example of what goes on in their own company every day. The participants leave the game with a newfound appreciation of their personal impact on the performance of the business. Employees create that line of sight between their daily activities and the performance of the company. And the experience of playing the game serves to focus their energy on improving business performance.

The game breaks a business down into four main components: sales, strategies, expenses, and receivables. It's a simple but effective representation of any business. All viable companies generate sales, implement business strategies, pay their bills, and get paid by their customers. That's basically it.

Let's look at each of these components in more detail.

Sales

A business cannot survive without sales. More important, a business cannot survive without profitable sales. The lesson is that employees have direct impact on whether a sale is profitable.

Most businesses are lucky to earn 5 to 7 cents in profit on $1 of revenue. Expenses such as the cost of goods sold, sales, general and administrative expenses, operational expenses, taxes, and interest take a big chunk out of a dollar of revenue. Therefore, effective execution is at a premium.

One slipup, one upset customer, a little extra waste on the shop floor, or some unexpected downtime on a piece of equipment can easily turn a profitable sale into a loss. Your employees need to understand this fact.

Employees who are accountable for customer satisfaction and who exercise initiative in controlling expenses can have a direct impact on the organization's profitability.

Strategies

New business strategies are the engine of business growth. You have to do new things in order to grow. If everyone did the same thing they did last year the business would perform exactly the same. You would generate that same 5 to 7 cents profit on $1 of revenue. But where would the salary increases come from? How would you invest in new equipment? How would you go after new opportunities?

Participants learn this first hand in the Risks and Rewards game. Participants have to decide on investment strategies—a training program for new employees, a new piece of equipment, or the strategic acquisition of a company. They learn that investing in new capabilities is the fastest way to improve the bottom line—but risk comes with every investment.

Not all investments pay off. It takes cash to invest. What if you don't have the cash available? Do you get a bank loan? These are important decisions that leaders make every day.

The bottom line is that the success of new business strategies is critical. Therefore, employees must know it is serious business when the boss asks for their participation on a new pilot team or other initiative. If the initiative fails, the entire organization suffers.

Employees who take the initiative to develop new capabilities are crucial to success. They have to be accountable for results. They have to be team players, give their best efforts to improving the company's performance, and focus externally in order to recognize new opportunities.

Expenses

How do the signs of growth relate to business expenses? Just consider what happens when it's time to pay for that new piece of equipment and there's no cash available. Focusing on business expenses helps employees understand the importance of cash.

Too often, managers make business decisions without considering cash flow. Cash management is usually someone else's responsibility. Managers just stay within their budgets and expect someone else to worry about paying the bills. This is the wrong approach.

When a company runs out of cash, it must go to the bank. Interest charges begin to pile up. There's an old saying: Companies don't go out of business because they are losing money, they go out of business when they don't have any money. Cash management is critically important.

Employees who take the initiative to consider cash in their decision-making processes do a valuable service for the customer. Employees who consider themselves accountable for cash flow add value. Cash is king.

Receivables

How quickly do you turn over receivables? In other words, how quickly do your customers pay your invoices? Receivable aging is an excellent predictor of customer satisfaction. If your customers aren't satisfied, they are likely to delay payment.

Employees can have a profound impact on receivable aging. Employees who focus on the customer ensure that the customer is happy. Ownership culture employees are accountable for getting invoices out as quickly as possible. They ensure that the accounting or billing department has the necessary information. They don't view it as somebody else's job to bill the customer—they ensure that the bills go out and get paid, and they exercise initiative in following up with slow-paying customers in order to resolve any unknown problems.

CONCLUSION

Potato farmers play a dangerous game as the harvest season approaches. They know that the longer the potatoes stay in the ground, the bigger they become. But they also know that a hard freeze can wipe out the entire crop if they wait too long. Harvest time is not the time to relax, it is a time to reap the rewards of a long and arduous process.

This is an apt analogy for building an ownership culture. It is a long and arduous process that requires tremendous vision, leadership, and hard work. As the signs of growth appear in your organization, you know that the harvest is coming. It's time to get ready to reap the rewards. But there's still work to be done.

Your employees demonstrate high levels of initiative, accountability, team spirit, and external focus. The trick is to help them understand enough about your business that they can put that positive energy to work improving it.

Help your employees draw that line of sight between their daily activities and your financial statements. When you do, you gather an abundant harvest.

Part 3

*An Ownership
Culture at Work*

Geoffrey Moore, author of *Crossing the Chasm*, defines a *discontinuous innovation* as a new product or service that requires the end user and the marketplace to dramatically change their past behavior with the promise of gaining equally dramatic new benefits.[1]

The Internet is an excellent example of a discontinuous innovation. It challenges our fundamental beliefs about communicating, gathering information, and even purchasing products and services. But the promise of the Internet is equally exciting—it opens new vistas of opportunity for individuals and businesses worldwide.

Moore describes how consumers segregate themselves along an axis of risk aversion when considering whether to adopt a new product. For example, some people are innovators, quick to avail themselves of a new opportunity. At the other end of the scale are the laggards. These are the risk-averse folks among us. Someone who still avoids using a personal computer might fall into this category. In the middle are the early adopters, the early majority, and the later majority. These folks willingly adopt new ideas when they are presented with a compelling reason to change their thinking.

Moore represents these categories of consumers graphically with a bell curve (Figure III.1). He calls this model the *technology adoption life cycle* (TALC) because it defines how new ideas or technologies are accepted over time. As the model shows, the innovators adopt an idea first, followed by the early adopters, then the early majority, the late majority, and finally (if ever) the laggards. The TALC also shows that most consumers fall into the early- and late-majority categories. Therefore, these consumer groups represent the largest market opportunity for a new product or service.

Moore postulates that producers of new technology must develop marketing programs based on the TALC model because it tracks the acceptance of new ideas. He offers a complete marketing approach for innovative technology products. It goes something like this:

- Offer the new product to the innovators, for free if necessary, so that they can help you educate the early adopters.
- When you capture the early adopters' attention, do whatever it takes to satisfy them so they serve as good references for the early majority.

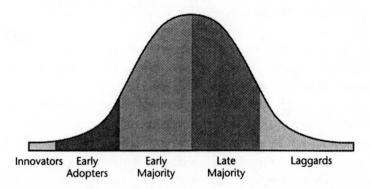

Figure III.1 Technology adoption life cycle (TALC). (From *Crossing the Chasm* by Geoffrey A. Moore. Copyright © 1991 by Geoffrey A. Moore. Reprinted by permission of HarperCollins Publishers, Inc.)

- Leverage the references of the early adopters to gain the bulk of your revenue by serving the early majority.
- Capitalize on your success with the early majority to prove to the later majority that your products are reliable and cheap enough for them to use.
- Ignore the laggards—they aren't worth the trouble.

Many household names in technology, including Microsoft, Oracle, and Lotus, have followed this recipe for success. The trick is in navigating the transition from marketing to the early adopters to marketing to the early majority, which Moore calls *crossing the chasm*. Most technology products that fail do so because they get trapped in the chasm, according to Moore.

THE PERIL OF THE CHASM

The transition in marketing from the early adopter to the early majority proves difficult because these two consumer groups are very different, although they fall next to each other in the TALC model. Early adopters are visionaries. They are people who see the possibilities of a new idea or technology before it is completely developed. They believe that they can achieve a dramatic competitive advantage over the status quo by being first to exploit a new capability.

On the other hand, the early and later majority are pragmatists. They look for proven solutions. They stick with the status quo until you give them a compelling reason to buy. To them, new ideas, technology, or approaches are valuable only when they establish a proven track record and a solid set of references.

So, how do you transition your marketing to the pragmatists? The answer, according to Moore, is *focus*. You target a pressing need in a specific niche market and ensure that you provide a complete solution to the problem. For example,

Apple Computers initially focused on desktop publishing applications for the Macintosh, Lotus initially focused on the account management function for its Lotus Notes software, and Peoplesoft focused on the human resource management function for its client/server-based enterprise resource management software.

Focus is required because developing the complete solutions that pragmatists demand is expensive and time-consuming. Pragmatists buy your new idea only when it completely solves a critical business problem for which there is no alternative solution.

Most companies stumble when they address too many applications at the same time. They run out of time or money before they can develop the track record necessary to win over the pragmatists. However, companies that practice the discipline of focus give themselves the opportunity to become a market leader in their chosen niche. Then they can leverage that leadership in other related markets until the innovation is accepted by the mainstream, leaving them with an undisputed competitive advantage.

Amazon.com, the pioneer of online bookselling, is a good example. It is leveraging its leadership in online bookselling to enter the online music and video markets. Amazon.com will be in a powerful competitive position as mainstream consumers accept online retailing.

OWNERSHIP CULTURE TECHNOLOGY

We reviewed Moore's TALC model because ownership culture can be considered a new organizational development technology. As such, it is reasonable to expect that the adoption of ownership culture follows Moore's pattern. Our experience in promoting ownership culture has in fact proven this.

We have talked with dozens of executives in industries ranging from high technology to consumer products. In some cases, executives immediately embraced the notion of an ownership culture. In other cases, the fear and uncertainty we stirred up was palpable. And in a few cases, we evoked outright disdain.

We discovered that many business leaders are not early adopters of new leadership ideas. Many leaders are laggards.

It's not that business leaders fail to recognize the importance of developing a highly skilled and motivated workforce, it's just that concepts like trust and coaching, open communication, and sharing information are out of character for many managers. Many leaders say, "I really see the value of building an ownership culture, but if I start trying some of these things, my employees will think I've lost my mind." We conclude that an adversarial relationship still exists between employees and management in many companies. Many leaders just accept employee turnover rates of 30 to 40 percent, as if they were a force of nature. But nothing could be further from the truth.

Although ownership culture makes good common sense to us, we found that many view it as a radical new leadership approach. Therefore, the TALC model and the discipline of crossing the chasm apply equally well to promoting the acceptance of ownership culture. This is the subject of Part III.

Chapter 10 describes a specific business application of an ownership culture. In the true spirit of crossing the chasm, we focus on just one application: attracting and retaining skilled workers. We hope to provide more evidence that the *Act Like an Owner* framework can solve your most pressing business problems.

Chapter 11 presents a larger historical context for the importance of an ownership culture. We illustrate the irony that businesses have worked to reduce their dependence on people for most of this century, only to find that people are more important to the success of a business than ever before as the twenty-first century approaches.

In essence, we conclude with a description of what lies on the other side of the chasm—business success in the twenty-first century.

10

Applying an Ownership Culture

Without a doubt, attracting top talent is a key business challenge for most organizations. But that's only half the problem—changing employee attitudes and expectations make it difficult to hold on to talented workers as well. In fact, the loss of talented workers forces many companies to reduce their growth projections and negatively affects their ability to compete.

The Time Value of People

The time value of money is a familiar concept. *Newsweek* financial writer Jane Bryant Quinn once said that the two most powerful forces in the world are gravity and the time value of money. The time value of money teaches you to start saving early in order to reach your financial goals, such as buying a house, sending your kids to college, or building a retirement nest egg. The earlier you start saving, the easier it is to achieve your goals.

We introduce the concept of the *time value of people* to quantify the importance of attracting and retaining people today.

Imagine that you must build a team of 10 people to develop a new product or provide services to a new customer account. What's the value of quickly building a top-notch team? The following equation helps determine the answer:

$$N = \left(\frac{52}{52 - D} * O\right) - O,$$

where $D =$ number of weeks it takes to staff open positions,

$O =$ number of open positions,

$N =$ number of additional people required due to the delay.

This formula shows that for each week of delay caused by the inability to find a suitable employee for an open position, you have to hire even more people just to stay even. Here's an example.

Suppose that it takes you an average of 16 weeks to fill an open position requiring a highly skilled individual (this is about average in many companies today). If you must build a team of 10 people who will develop a new product, the delay of 16 weeks (assuming that you have the capability to hire 10 people at the same time) means that you now need to hire almost 15 people to accomplish the same amount of work in the same period of time. Otherwise you need to delay the rollout of the new product. That's the time value of people.

Let's put a number on it.

If you can characterize the value in revenue potential or opportunity cost of a number of people working for a certain amount of time, this formula helps you calculate a dollar value for the time value of people (TVP):

$$\text{TVP} = V - \frac{V(W - D)}{W},$$

where V = value in revenue potential or opportunity cost of a team of people working W weeks on a project,

D = number of weeks it takes to build the team,

W = number of weeks the team works together on the project.

Let's assume that a team of 10 people servicing a new customer account for a full year is worth $1.5 million in revenue to your business. If it takes 10 weeks to pull the team together, what is the cost in terms of TVP? Using the formula

$$TVP = \$1{,}500{,}000 - \frac{\$1{,}500{,}000(52 - 10)}{52} = \$288{,}462.$$

In other words, the delay of 10 weeks costs you $288,462 unless you can figure out a way to get the work done faster. It's true that this revenue is only *delayed*—you make it up eventually, assuming that you can find the people you need. But at what cost? Did you lose your time-to-market advantage over a competitor? Are your customers upset that their project is delayed? Those losses are priceless. There's no getting around the fact that TVP is critically important.

So how does an ownership culture help you solve the TVP problem? Let's look at the recruiting and retention problem in a slightly different way.

A MARKETING PROBLEM

Consider that the problem of attracting and retaining top talent is not merely an operational problem, or even a human resource problem—it is a *marketing* problem. Let us explain.

Philip Kottler, the well-known marketing academic, defines a *product* as anything offered to a market that satisfies a consumer want or need.[1] He goes further to define five levels of a product:

1.   *The core product level.*   The fundamental need or want that the product satisfies for the consumer.

2.   *The generic product level.*   The basic, no-frills version of the product.

3.   *The expected product level.*   The set of product attributes and features that consumers normally expect when they buy the product.

4.   *The augmented product level.*   The set of attributes that go above and beyond consumers' normal expectations. These are the features and benefits that differentiate a product.

5.   *The potential product level.*   The set of all possible future transformations of the product.

Consider a basic mobile phone. At the core product level, the fundamental need is mobile communications. Therefore, the generic product level specifies a mobile phone that simply allows the user to make and receive phone calls. But most consumers want more than that from a mobile phone. That's where the expected product level comes in.

At the expected product level, consumers demand features such as storage capacity for frequently called numbers, reasonably wide service area, reasonable battery life, backlit screen for night use, compact size, and reasonable sound quality.

At the augmented product level, attributes like digital transmission and integrated paging and voice mail services are desirable. And at the potential product level, the ability to make or receive a phone call anywhere in the world, the ability to access the Internet via the phone, and automatic call routing that allows you to dial one phone number and reach someone at home, at the office, or on the road are conceivable.

The salient point of this discussion is that products succeed or fail at the augmented product level. Most manufacturers can produce a satisfactory product at the expected product level; the only way to effectively differentiate a product is to augment it with additional features. But there's a catch-22 involved here.

Smart product developers understand that they must deliver more than the consumer expects. However, they often fall into a trap that David Aaker, author of *Building Strong Brands,* calls the *product attribute trap.*[2] Competing product developers engage in product attribute competition that ends up differentiating no one. Consider this example.

Two manufacturers of mobile phones compete at the augmented product level. The first manufacturer adds the capability to store 10 frequently called numbers. So the second manufacturer provides for storage of 20 phone numbers. Not to be outdone, the first manufacturer introduces a new model that stores 30 numbers. And so it goes.

Which is the better phone? Which stands out—the capability to store 20 numbers or 30 numbers? To most consumers, neither one. Most consumers are satisfied if the phone holds 10 or 15 numbers. Anything above that no longer matters, so it doesn't differentiate the product.

Over the long run, it is impossible to differentiate a product by simply adding features. New features are too easy to copy, and they fail to differentiate competing products that are considered satisfactory for the particular attribute under evaluation.

So how do you deal with the paradox that you must compete at the augmented product level, but you won't stand out if you merely add more features? The answer is in the type of features and attributes you associate with your products.

New features can be tangible functions, such as the capability to store frequently used phone numbers, or they can be intangible features that are not directly related to the product at all. For example, such diverse features as packaging, pricing, product endorsements, advertising, sales locations and distribution channels, and image are all relevant attributes. In fact, a product's intangible attributes are all that truly differentiate it at the augmented product level.

Products become brands at the augmented product level, because the intangible attributes of the product are a central component of its value proposition to the consumer. Products and brands are not the same thing.

A *product* is anything that can be offered to a market to satisfy a customer's need or want. A *brand* is a product that adds other attributes, especially intangible ones, to differentiate it in some way from competitive products that satisfy the same need. The intangibles differentiate—that's the lesson you need when you try to stand out as an employer of choice.

A Job, a Product, or a Brand?

The availability of top talent is just not keeping up with demand. The tables have turned—the employee is in charge. Companies don't *interview* anymore, they *sell*. You must view the jobs you offer prospective employees as products. Then you can use Kottler's five product levels to differentiate your organization's ownership culture in the eyes of prospective employees.

At the core product level, a job provides a paycheck. This is the basic need or want that employees satisfy by getting a job. But most employees today expect more, so we find health benefits, paid vacation time, educational benefits, and many other perquisites at the expected product level.

At the augmented product level, we often find features such as stock options, bonus plans, on-site day care, and a host of other creative compensation and benefit programs.

At the potential product level, a job is much more than a paycheck—it provides fulfillment and meaning; it is a vocation or a calling.

Your goal is to differentiate the job opportunities you offer prospective employees. Unfortunately, many employers fall into the same product attribute trap that manufacturers of consumer products do.

Most hiring managers identify higher salaries, more benefits, stock options, and more training as prototypical methods of recruiting and retaining employees. But these are just product attributes. Your competitors can copy what you are doing, and someone always outbids you. You are not addressing the most important needs of your customers, in this case your employees.

Remember, employees of the companies at the top of *Fortune's* list of the 100 best places to work never mention money when they are asked why they stay. Time and again, these surveys show that employees want more than a good-paying job.

The only way to become an employer of choice is to differentiate yourself at the augmented product level by relying on the intangible benefits of working for your organization. This means that your corporate culture becomes the key differentiating factor in the hiring equation. Your corporate culture encapsulates the intangible benefits of working for your organization. The positions, titles, roles, and jobs you offer your employees are your products. Your corporate culture is your *brand*.

The Benefits of Branding Your Workplace

Branding is a marketing technique that matches a product or service offering with a specific target market. The goal is to cultivate a loyal customer base that values the attributes and characteristics associated with the product.

You offer employees empowerment, fulfillment, opportunity, and respect when you adopt an ownership culture. And you attract entrepreneurial employees who exhibit initiative, accountability, team spirit, and customer focus.

The ownership culture brand is designed to appeal to this target market. When word gets out in the industry that your company offers an ownership culture, you create pull within your target market, attracting the caliber of employee you desire.

One business leader found that prospective employees who interviewed with his company often brought along a magazine article about his company and its efforts to build an ownership culture. Prospective employees routinely referred to that article and indicated that they wanted to be part of a company that embraced such ideas. When employees seek you out and your retention rates skyrocket, you know the full power of the ownership culture brand.

CONCLUSION

Your ownership culture is as important to your ability to attract and retain the talented people you need as the Pampers brand is to Procter & Gamble's ability to sell disposable diapers. Stay focused on the intangible aspects of working for your company. It's the best way to leverage the time value of people and stand out as an employer of choice.

11

*What Goes Around
Comes Around*

According to recent surveys conducted by Watson Wyatt Worldwide and Coopers and Lybrand Consulting, CEOs believe that the following issues will be critical to the success of their organizations over the next two to three years:[1]

- *Development of leadership talent.* CEOs believe that the ability to lead people is the most important skill managers need. They also believe that poor leadership is the primary cause of business failure.
- *Growth of employee knowledge.* CEOs believe that increased worker knowledge and skills are important in improving financial results. Innovative, motivated, and involved employees are absolutely critical.
- *Pay for performance.* CEOs are concerned that pay has become an entitlement. They are eager to recast compensation programs as part of a larger strategy to motivate and engage employees in a manner that drives improvements to the bottom line.
- *Communication between management and employees.* CEOs strongly believe that communication is one of the top

ways to increase employee productivity and improve
financial performance.
• *Creation of an environment of shared values.* CEOs
believe that the creation of a strong corporate culture
that shifts employee attitudes and behavior to embrace
accountability will best improve financial performance.
They believe that an environment of shared values and
goals is second only to communication as a strategy for
enhancing performance.

In essence, the corporate executives surveyed place *people*
at the crux of their strategies for success in a rapidly changing
and competitive business climate. They understand that a
great product or service and solid execution no longer suffice
in the current business environment. Success is currently
determined by how well you can align, inspire, and mobilize
people around a business strategy. The new goal is to mobilize
human intellect and ingenuity for competitive advantage.

The globalization of the economy over the last 20 years
has forced companies across the world to reorganize both
their structural and financial capital to achieve a competitive edge. But to reach the next level of performance, companies must focus on their human capital—their people.

That's why the *act like an owner* (ALO) model is an idea
whose time has come. The ALO model directly addresses
each of the concerns identified by CEOs in the surveys we
cited. Let's review.

DEVELOPMENT OF LEADERSHIP TALENT

ALO is all about leadership. We described the role of the
leader as a *coach* in Chapter 8. The second C in COACH
stands for *creating next-generation leaders.* ALO leaders not
only constantly improve their own leadership skills, they
diligently work to identify and develop next-generation

leaders. ALO leaders know that the future of the company depends on leadership. They act as stewards of the company as they develop next-generation leaders.

GROWTH OF EMPLOYEE KNOWLEDGE

The growth of employee knowledge begins with defining your operating model, as we described in Chapter 3. When you model your business along the customer, economic, business parameter, and core process dimensions, you build consensus on how your business works and earns money, and you establish a framework for teaching everyone in the company how they impact business performance. You know that poor performance is the result of ignorance, not negligence.

Teaching people how the business works is one of the principles and values in your culture (it is the first *T* in the TRUST mnemonic introduced in Chapter 5). You look for potential employees' ability to learn your operating model, to teach your operating model, and to improve your operating model. You view mistakes as tuition payments—valuable learning opportunities. You create a learning organization.

PAY FOR PERFORMANCE

We discussed compensation and reward in Chapters 5 and 6. *Reward* is the *R* in the TRUST mnemonic.

Every employee has a stake in the outcome in an ownership culture. Their reward is tied to the performance of the business and their contribution to that performance. ALO leaders develop compensation programs that motivate the appropriate behaviors (thinking and acting like an owner), they ensure that everyone understands how results are measured, and they apply the measurements consistently to everyone in the organization. Appropriate, clear, and consistent reward systems are a powerful way to motivate and engage employees in a manner that drives improvements to the bottom line and achieves pay for performance.

COMMUNICATION BETWEEN MANAGEMENT AND EMPLOYEES

The first C in the COACH mnemonic means *communication*. ALO leaders constantly communicate messages about the customer, the company, and the future. They know that what they say has a profound impact on the behavior of their employees and on their perceived leadership abilities. Communication skills are at a premium in ALO organizations.

CREATION OF AN ENVIRONMENT OF SHARED VALUES

An ownership culture is the heart of the ALO model. It is a corporate culture that embraces the principles and values of the entrepreneur. The TRUST mnemonic describes the basic values shared by everyone in the ALO organization; it is the value proposition offered to employees.

An ownership culture also values initiative, accountability, team spirit, and customer focus (Chapter 7). These are the signs that an ownership culture is at work in your organization. And as we described in Chapter 8, leadership, communication, and creating a higher purpose are equally important in an ownership culture.

TRUST, initiative, accountability, team spirit, customer focus, communication, leadership, empowerment, and purpose are the shared values of an ownership culture. Making these values part of your culture to ensure that everyone in your organization embraces them is a powerful performance-enhancing strategy. The ALO model is clearly an idea whose time has come.

CONCLUSION

It's been said that the conflict in a good story plot is like a train wreck. Two trains speed toward each other from far away. The farther apart they begin, the better. The greater their momentum, the more spectacular the impact.

The trains in the drama of business are the twentieth and twenty-first centuries. They are on a collision course. The conflict is human capital versus financial capital. The conflict has been brewing since the end of the nineteenth century when our country began its transitioning from an agricultural to an industrial society.

Our agricultural society relied upon human capital. The independent family farmer relied on instinct, raw courage, and the support of family and community to survive.

In the industrial era, the focus shifted to financial capital. After World War II, the insatiable demand of a growing population produced a golden era for U.S. businesses. Large business conglomerates driven by centralized planning and market research emerged. Their goal was scalability—the ability to enter new, growing markets and produce just enough product to satisfy demand. Size meant power.

As population growth slowed and global competition heated up, the focus shifted to competitive strategy (à la Michael Porter). Differentiation and focus became the watchwords as companies accepted the business environment as a given and concentrated on market position. Size was still a deciding factor as companies erected barriers to entry in their markets.

Then the wheels came off the cart in the 1960s and 1970s. Global competition overtook U.S. business. Quality and continuous improvement became the vogue, and U.S. businesses needed to catch up. Companies designed themselves around their core competencies—reengineering and right-sizing became the tools of choice.

Now the information revolution is taking us back to our roots. The information era is characterized by the entrepreneur. Small- and medium-sized businesses now fuel the growth of the U.S. economy.

The small business owner is the hero of the modern U.S. economy. The entrepreneur has replaced the corporate manager as our role model. Today's successful entrepreneur relies on instinct, raw courage, and the support of a dedicated team of employees to succeed—not unlike the family farmer of a century ago. What goes around, comes around.

It's time for the grand finale in the drama of twentieth-century business. It's financial capital versus human capital, and we'll soon know who wins. But all indications are that the winning businesses in the next century will be those that understand how to mobilize human intellect and ingenuity for competitive advantage. Adopting the principle presented in *Act Like an Owner* is the best way to ensure that you end up on the side of the winners.

Notes

Part 1

[1]Statistics from general literature provided by the International Franchise Association.

[2]Adrian Slywotsky, *Value Migration* (Boston: Harvard Business School Press, 1996), p. 14.

Chapter 1

[1]James Kouzes and Barry Posner, *The Leadership Challenge* (San Francisco: Jossey-Bass, 1987), pp. 16–21.

Chapter 2

[1]John Kotter and James Heskett, *Corporate Culture and Performance* (New York: The Free Press, 1992), pp. 15–57.

Part 2

Chapter 5

[1]Noel Tichy, *The Leadership Engine* (New York: HarperCollins, 1997), p. 12.

[2]Ken Blanchard, et al., *Empowerment Takes More Than a Minute*, (San Francisco: Berrett-Koehler, 1996), p. 78.

Chapter 7

[1]Max DePree, *Leadership is an Art*, (New York: Dell, 1989), pp. 45–51.

[2]Gary Hamel and C. K. Prahalad, *Competing for the Future* (Boston: Harvard Business School Press, 1994), pp. 3–5.

Chapter 8

[1]James Kouzes and Barry Posner, *The Leadership Challenge* (San Francisco: Jossey-Bass, 1987), pp. 7–14.

[2]Ken Blanchard, et al., *The One Minute Manager Builds High Performing Teams* (New York: William Morren and Company, 1991), pp. 31–64.

[3]John Kotter, *Leading Change* (Boston: Harvard Business School Press, 1996), pp. 33–145.

Part 3

[1]Geoffrey Moore, *Crossing the Chasm* (New York: HarperBusiness, 1991), pp. 10–11.

Chapter 10

[1]Theodore Levitt, "Marketing Success through Differentiation—of Anything," *Harvard Business Review*, January–February 1980, pp. 83–91.

[2]David Aaker, *Building Strong Brands* (New York: The Free Press, 1996), pp. 72–76.

Chapter 11

[1]Watson Wyatt Worldwide, press release, 9 December 1997; Coopers and Lybrand Consulting, press release, 10 December 1997.

Index

About the Authors

Robert Blonchek is CEO of Bottom Line Staffing Solutions, a contract engineering firm specializing in the information technology industry. He is a frequent contributing author, speaker, and consultant on the *Act Like an Owner* model and its implications for business and career planning. He lives near Baltimore, Maryland, with his wife and three children.

Martin O'Neill is President and CEO of CTX Corporation, a knowledge engineering company that is another working example of an ownership culture and entrepreneurial employees in action. He is a speaker and consultant on leading corporate change by implementing the *Act Like an Owner* model. He lives near Annapolis, Maryland, with his wife and two sons.

Printed in the United States
105783LV00002B/130-138/A

9 780471 322856